P9-DGS-414

Twayne's United States Authors Series

Sylvia E. Bowman, *Editor*

INDIANA UNIVERSITY

Edith Wharton

TUSAS 265

Courtesy American Academy of Arts and Letters

Edith Wharton

EDITH WHARTON

By MARGARET B. MC DOWELL
University of Iowa

TWAYNE PUBLISHERS
A DIVISION OF G. K. HALL & CO., BOSTON

CARNEGIE LIBRARY
LIVINGSTONE COLLEGE
SALISBURY, N. C. 28144

Copyright © 1976 by G. K. Hall & Co.

All Rights Reserved

First Printing

Library of Congress Cataloging in Publication Data

McDowell, Margaret Louise Blaine, 1923-
  Edith Wharton.

  (Twayne's United States authors series ; TUSAS 265
  Bibliography: p. 149 - 55.
  Includes index.
    1. Wharton, Edith Newbold Jones, 1862-1937 —
  Criticism and interpretation.
  PS3545.H16Z745   813'.5'2   75-44094
  ISBN 0-8057-7164-6

MANUFACTURED IN THE UNITED STATES OF AMERICA

813.52
W553

To my husband

99368

Contents

About the Author

Margaret B. McDowell is chairperson of the Women's Studies Program and an associate professor of Rhetoric at the University of Iowa. A summa cum laude graduate of Coe College, she received the M.A. in creative writing and the Ph.D. in English from the University of Iowa. She formerly taught at Kansas State College, Pittsburg, and at MacMurray College, Jacksonville, Illinois. She is a member of the executive commitees of the Women's Caucus for the Modern Languages and of the Midwest Modern Language Association and has been vice-chairman of the University of Iowa Faculty Council and Faculty Senate.

Her other writing on Edith Wharton includes articles on the ghost tales, the short story techniques, and the feminist values in Wharton's fiction. She is also the author of essays on the rhetoric of the Women's Movement, on sexism in language, on the teaching of language arts to children, on children's literature, and on college composition. Currently she is writing a critical work about Carson McCullers for the Twayne United States Authors Series.

Preface

Mrs. Wharton's work is so important, so varied, and so extensive that it justifies renewed considerations and appraisals. Thirty-five years after her death, her place in the history of 'American literature is secure. Other than a recognition of her mastery in the short story and a recognition of *The House of Mirth, Ethan Frome, The Custom of the Country*, and *The Age of Innocence* as her masterpieces, there is, however, little consensus as to the relative importance of the rest of her extensive canon.

Before *The House of Mirth*, Edith Wharton's novellas, her books on houses and gardens, and her short stories were widely reviewed; and the authentic details of her historical novel, *The Valley of Decision*, impressed scholars and critics. Reviews of her short stories tended to emphasize her technical adroitness and her epigrammatic flair rather than her perceptive explorations of human nature. The success of *The House of Mirth* established her as an important writer whose future promised much. Her long and affectionate friendship with Henry James bore fruit in her own work, particularly in the disciplined artistry revealed in *Madame de Treymes* and *The Reef*. The stark realism and relentless irony characterizing *Ethan Frome* rather surprisingly won a large audience in an age when many readers still preferred the pleasures of romance. In the same mode of sardonic realism, *The Custom of the Country* established her as a notable practitioner of the comedy of manners, a reputation confirmed in the 1920's by *The Age of Innocence, Twilight Sleep*, and *The Children*. Her satiric brilliance shines in each of these books.

Mrs. Wharton's European residence after 1912 and the long interval elapsing between *The Custom of the Country* (1913) and *The Age of Innocence* (1920) diminished interest in her work. *The Age of Innocence*, though some readers recognized it as a masterpiece, provoked mixed reactions among its readers because Mrs. Wharton focused in it on an earlier time and on the inner lives of the New York aristocracy when *Main Street* was the most widely read serious novel in America. *A Son at the Front*, despite its real merits as a novel and social document, evoked negative reactions because the public was no longer interested in reading about the war that had just concluded. *Glimpses of the Moon* and *The Mother's Recompense* were weak novels and deserved the opprobrium that greeted them. However, it became a cliché judgment to proclaim, after the appearance of these novels, that Edith Wharton's work of consequence ended with *The Age of Innocence*.

But Edith Wharton never lost her status as a major writer, even after younger writers began to take precedence over her. A more focused revival of interest has followed the compilation of essays in Irving Howe's *Edith Wharton: A Collection of Critical Essays* (1962) and the publication of R. W. B. Lewis's *The Collected Short Stories of Edith Wharton* (1968). Several notable critiques of her work have recently appeared. Blake Nevius's *Edith Wharton: A Study of her Fiction* (1953), Louis Auchincloss's *Edith Wharton* (1961), and Geoffrey Walton's *Edith Wharton: A Critical Interpretation* (1970) are all discerning studies that have contributed much to our understanding and appreciation of her work. But no one has said the last word about her writing. The official biography by R. W. B. Lewis, *Edith Wharton* (1975), is based partly on the papers at Yale University which were not previously available. It contributes immeasurably to an accurate account of the events in her life.

In discussing Wharton's shorter fiction, I have been necessarily selective and have chosen for individual analysis only a few of the short stories and four of the novellas. I have examined in detail only the best of the several books growing out of her war experience, *A Son at the Front*. The two inferior novels written for the *Pictorial Review* in the 1920's, *Glimpses of the Moon* and *The Mother's Recompense*, I have mentioned only in passing.

Otherwise, I have sought to be inclusive, rather than exclusive, in my consideration of the works. While I concur with the general opinion that *The House of Mirth, Ethan Frome, The Custom of the Country,* and *The Age of Innocence* are Edith Wharton's masterpieces, I hope also to encourage the reading of several novels, novellas, and short stories that have received less attention. By providing extensive analysis and comment on her fiction after 1920, I want to show that, contrary to popular opinion, Edith Wharton continued to develop and to explore with versatility new genres,

Preface

techniques, and subject materials until a few weeks before her death in 1937 and that her continued interest in both American and European society after World War I provides an added dimension to her late work. If no single book after 1920 can be considered great, much that is notable in her prolific later work merits recognition, analysis, and appreciation.

My inclusive approach will, I hope, result in a clearer recognition of the extent of Edith Wharton's achievement and in a clearer recognition of her versatility and range. One emerges from a detailed study of her total work with an increased respect for her place in the American tradition as a realist who was a fastidious artist and a compassionate observer of the human scene.

Margaret B. McDowell

University of Iowa

Acknowledgments

I am indebted to the Old Gold Foundation of the University of Iowa and the Graduate College of the University of Iowa for providing me with an Old Gold Summer Faculty Research Fellowship to complete my work on this book.

I owe much to my husband, Frederick P. W. McDowell, for his criticism of my manuscript at various stages and for his shared appreciation of the works of Edith Wharton.

Acknowledgment is made to Charles Scribner's Sons for permission to reprint from these books by Edith Wharton: *The House of Mirth* (1904), *The Fruit of the Tree* (1907), *Ethan Frome* (1911), "Introduction" to The Modern Students Library Edition of *Ethan Frome* (1922), *Fighting France, from Dunkerque to Belfort* (1915), *The Custom of the Country* (1913), *A Son at the Front* (1922), and *The Writing of Fiction* (1925).

Acknowledgment is made to A. Watkins, Inc., for permission to reprint from the following books by Edith Wharton: *Summer* (1917), *The Age of Innocence* (1920), *Twilight Sleep* (1927), *The Children* (1928), *Hudson River Bracketed* (1929), *The Gods Arrive* (1932), *The Buccaneers* (1938), and *A Backward Glance* (1934).

Acknowledgment is made to the *Yale Review* for permission to quote from Edith Wharton, "The Great American Novel," XVI (July, 1927), 655.

Acknowledgment is made to Appleton-Century-Crofts for permission to quote from Percy Lubbock, *Portrait of Edith Wharton* (1947).

Chronology

1862   Edith Newbold Jones born January 24; 14 W. 23rd St., New York City; parents, George F. and Lucretia Stevens Rhinelander Jones.

1866 - 1872   Travelled in Europe with family.

1872 - 1879   Spent winters in New York; summers in Newport.

1879   Had debut, Fifth Avenue, New York.

1880 - 1882   Travelled in France and Italy.

1882   Death of father.

1882 - 1885   Lived with mother in New York and Newport.

1884   Met Walter Berry.

1885   Married Edward R. Wharton.

1888   Chartered yacht to cruise Aegean three months. Spent springs in Italy during early marriage. Lived in Pencraig and Land's End, Newport.

1891 - 1893   Two stories published. Wrote "Bunner Sisters."

1897   *Decoration of Houses* published with Ogden Codman.

1899   *The Greater Inclination.*

1900   *The Touchstone.*

1901   *Crucial Instances.* Built The Mount, Lenox, Massachusetts.

1902   *Valley of Decision;* translation of Herman Sudermann's *Es lebe das leben* published. Met Henry James.

1903   *Sanctuary.* Husband suffered mental illness.

1904   *Descent of Man and Other Stories; Italian Villas and Their Gardens.*

1905	*Italian Backgrounds; The House of Mirth.*
1907	*Madam de Treymes, A Motor Flight Through France, The Greater Inclination,* and *The Fruit of the Tree* published. Edward Wharton, Henry James, and Edith Wharton toured Western and Southern France. Husband suffered severe breakdown. Moved winter home from New York to 58 Rue de Varenne, Paris, an apartment rented from George Vanderbilt.
1908	*The Hermit and the Wild Woman.* Visited Henry James in London.
1909	Moved to 53 Rue de Varenne in Faubourg Saint-Germain; lived here until 1920. *Artemis to Acteon* published.
1910	*Tales of Men and Ghosts.* Edward Wharton suffered further breakdown.
1911	*Ethan Frome.* Separated from Edward Wharton. Sold The Mount, the Lenox, Massachusetts, residence.
1912	*The Reef.*
1913	*The Custom of the Country.* Started the novel to be called *Literature.* Divorced. Travelled in Germany with Bernard Berenson.
1914	Travelled to Algiers, Cantantine, and Tunis with Percy Lubbock and Gaillard Lapsley. In Majorca with Walter Berry when war began. Briefly in England. Returned to Paris. Organized war relief.
1915	*Fighting France.*
1916	*The Book of the Homeless.* Took charge of six hundred Belgian orphans. Death of Henry James.
1917	*Summer; Xingu and Other Stories.* Awarded Order of Leopold by Belgium. Made member of French Legion of Honor. Travelled three weeks in Morocco as guest of French government and the Resident General of Morocco.
1918	*The Marne.* Bought Pavillon Calombe, an eighteenth-century house in village near Paris.
1919	*French Ways and Their Meaning.*
1920	*In Morocco; The Age of Innocence.* Restored medieval monastery at Hyèris on the Riviera for summer home.
1921	Awarded Pulitzer Prize for *The Age of Innocence.*
1922	*Glimpses of the Moon.*
1923	*A Son at the Front.* First woman awarded Doctor of Letters by Yale University. Only trip to America after 1912.
1924	*Old New York.*

Chronology

1925	*The Mother's Recompense; The Writing of Fiction.*
1926	*Twelve Poems; Here and Beyond.* Chartered yacht for trip to Aegean to repeat the one taken in 1888.
1927	*Twilight Sleep.* Death of Walter Berry.
1928	*The Children.* Death of Edward Wharton.
1929	*Hudson River Bracketed.* Serious illness.
1930	*Certain People.* Elected to the American Academy of Arts and Letters.
1932	*The Gods Arrive.*
1933	*Human Nature.*
1934	*A Backward Glance.*
1936	*The World Over.*
1937	*Ghosts; The Buccaneers.* Died August 11 following a stroke. Buried in the Cimetière des Gonards at Versailles next to ashes of Walter Berry. Papers left to Yale University with stipulation that publication be withheld until 1968.

CHAPTER 1

Edith Wharton: Woman and Artist

I A Glance Backward:
the Child and the Young Woman

E DITH Wharton (1862 - 1937) is the most distinguished woman
writer America produced before 1940, but she was middle-aged
before her first important novel, *The House of Mirth* (1905),
appeared. In her autobiography, *A Backward Glance* (1934), she
reveals that a sensuous response to nature and to architecture, a love
of books, a fascination for imagining stories, an excitement in travel,
an ability to hold the ugly detail alongside the beautiful, and a concern for the powerless and inarticulate individual were all elements
that characterized her childhood. Later they dominated her life and
work.

Her relatives, mostly wealthy merchants, bankers, and lawyers,
came from families whose names Washington Irving mentioned in
his accounts of Hudson River history. Her family lived in Europe
during most of her childhood to avoid the inflation that followed the
Civil War. Possessing independent incomes, the men were pleasure
lovers and indulged in sea fishing, boat racing, and hunting; the
women presided over elaborate dinner parties. Though Edith Wharton treated these aristocrats with as much satire as sympathy, she
asserted in her autobiography that they upheld high standards in
education, exemplified good manners, and observed "scrupulous
probity" in business and private affairs.

Edith Wharton's biographers depict her as an energetic and
sociable aristocrat in America and abroad and as a friend of notable
men. But they also note that she was a slightly alienated observer;
she was aloof in her earlier years from old New York society and disdainful in her later years of the literary fashion and of the intellectual
chaos of the 1920's and 1930's. A dominating woman, she swept

Henry James through a whirlwind of activities, conveyed to her publishers and reviewers her expectations of them, and took full charge during World War I of six hundred refugee children. But she was also reticent and painfully sensitive to criticism. She realized with anguish that her relatives did not approve her divorce, that her friendship with Walter Berry had become a subject for gossip, and that many of her later readers and critics were rejecting her approach to literature and life as genteel, mannered, and outdated. She was vulnerable from the first and felt an increasing sense of alienation with the years.

Edith Wharton's marriage, with its early and unresolved sexual disappointments, became excruciating as she saw her husband after 1903 fall victim to mental illness. She was twenty-three when she married thirty-five-year-old Edward (Teddy) Wharton, whose family figured in Boston and Philadelphia society. Though he did not share her intellectual interests or literary ambitions, he did share her love for travel. In her autobiography she curiously referred to her wedding in 1885 less in terms of gratified love than in terms of satisfied wanderlust: "At the end of my second winter in New York I was married; and thenceforth my thirst for travel was to be gratified" (90).[1] Three years after marriage, the Whartons planned a four-month cruise of the Aegean, which entailed an expenditure considered reckless by their relatives. Edith hesitated because of the opposition of both families, but Teddy decided the matter. At least she owed to her husband this cruise which she described in 1934 as "the greatest step forward in my making."

In the early years of their marriage, the Whartons spent the spring in Italy; and for some fifteen years they left each autumn for Europe. During the early 1890's Edith Wharton began suffering from a recurring and severe depressive illness, but she had won recovery from it by 1902, when her husband's mental illness became evident. After the success of *The Decoration of Houses* (1897) and the publication of some two dozen short stories and a few poems, Edith Wharton in the late 1890's wished to meet other authors and thought that she had to travel to do so. At the same time, she began to realize that her writing required disciplined, uninterrupted effort. From 1900 to 1911, The Mount, a country house she designed and built at Lenox, Massachusetts, provided freedom from social pressures, allowed her to write steadily each morning, and, incidentally, gratified her love of nature. Later she looked back with satisfaction upon her New England decade.

She would have been content to make her permanent home there but for her husband's health, his need for more stimulating surroundings or a warmer climate, and financial instability as a result of his medical expenses. For ten years the Whartons spent winters either in a New York or Paris apartment and summers and autumns at The Mount. Had Mrs. Wharton been able to choose freely, she would have preferred an English to a Parisian winter residence, but Teddy needed a mild climate. Only after she had to sell The Mount in 1911 did she make the Paris apartment in the Rue de Varenne her year-round home. In 1918 she restored the Pavillon Colombe in St. Brice-sous-Forêt, twelve miles north of Paris. In 1920 it became her residence during the rest of her life except for many winters spent in the convent near Hyèris, Ste. Claire du Vieux Château, which she leased and restored.

II   *The Friendship with Walter Berry*

When Edith Wharton met Walter Berry in 1884, she was recovering from the embarrassment of an engagement broken after its public announcement. For a few weeks she and Berry were together; then chance separated them until 1897, twelve years after her marriage to Wharton. The early encounter with Berry was crucial for Edith Wharton because it revealed to her that sexual attraction could coexist with intellectual stimulus and satisfaction. Berry was a wealthy lawyer, three years older than she; and he was later the friend of Henry James, Marcel Proust, and other notables. After several years in international law, he became judge of the international tribunal in Cairo from 1909 to 1916 and was president of the American Chamber of Commerce in Paris from 1916 to 1923.

For over thirty years, Mrs. Wharton's relationship with Berry proved a source both of inspiration and anguish to the sensitive and emotional woman. She was sure of her affection for him, but, unfortunately, she could not be sure of his for her. He never married. While her autobiography suggests that Berry almost alone gave her confidence as an aspiring writer, the uncertainty in their relationship produced frustration that sometimes shook her confidence. Whether they lived together at any time, the conclusion is inescapable that for years she sublimated her devotion for him and that she found in him her closest companionship. After her divorce, she asserted that she had hardly felt her previous suffering because she had willed herself to live apart in a world of her own creation. Walter Berry must have figured in this willed existence. After she left America permanently in 1911 to live in Europe, Berry provided a focus for her life. During long separations they corresponded actively, she sent her manuscripts regularly to him for criticism, and they read the same books. Berry was skilled in several languages; and, like Edith Wharton, he read insatiably in science, history, biography, travel, and archeology. They discussed new books as they discovered them, and she thought his reading of poetry intense and memorable. They were returning from Majorca together when World War I broke out, a trip James referred to as that of "another George Sand and another Chopin." At one point they toured the front lines together with French officials. After the war until Berry's death in 1927, they were close companions and frequently travelled together. When she moved to her new homes, Ste. Claire and Pavillon Calombe, in 1920, Berry leased the apartment in the Rue de Varenne, which had been her home from 1910. She sometimes presided as his hostess here.

Bachelors or ineffectual husbands appear frequently in her fiction — characters who love books and art, who often seem worthy of love, but who never commit themselves to a woman. Critics have speculated that Berry served as prototype for these men and that her ambiguous treatment of them may reflect her varying love and resentment during the thirty years of close companionship. There is no doubt about the sexual magnetism of these men, whose moral strength varies from figure to figure. Berry may have been no more committed than these characters, but he had a more vital intelligence. Seven years after his death, she summarized all that he had meant to her as a person and as a thinker: "No words can say, because such things are unsayable, how the influence of his thought, his character, his deepest personality, were interwoven with mine" (115).

Walter Berry's criticism may have had more immediate effect upon her work than Henry James's, for Berry helped her from the beginning. His hand was strong in *The Decoration of Houses* (1897), her first full-scale book. This book was the result of the Whartons' buying an old house at Newport, "Land's End," which they remodelled, decorated, and furnished simply in reaction to opulent Victorian fashion. Edith Wharton and Ogden Codman, a Boston architect, not only planned the decoration but also the book which sets forth a philosophy of interior design that stresses simplicity, proportion, and balance. French and Italian eighteenth-century houses, English Georgian and Queen Anne revivals, and American

Colonial mansions (like The Mount which Edith Wharton later designed) were supplanting the monotonous brownstone house. To her distress, builders of these new houses designed interiors that were incompatible with the exteriors; the builders overlooked the function of the rooms and used indiscriminately draperies, heavy furniture, and cheap imitation period furnishings. In this book she provides plans for bedrooms, dens, ballrooms, music rooms, libraries, nurseries, and school rooms; and she professes her preferences for fireplaces, candlelit drawing rooms, and eighteenth-century furniture.

Before the book found a publisher, Berry worked several weeks with Mrs. Wharton and molded her "lump" into clear English. In these weeks, she maintained, she learned from him whatever she was to know of clear, concise English. This pattern of semicollaborative writing continued for over thirty years. She poured out her work with relative freedom and then counted on the patient Berry to go over her manuscripts sentence by sentence for problems of syntax, metaphor, overemphasis, and repetition. With Berry insisting on concision and austerity, they went "adjective-hunting" and eliminated unnecessary words or phrases. Berry also decided, at least in the early collections, which short stories were to be reprinted in book form. When she bogged down in writing *The Valley of Decision* (1902), he told her to write everything that occurred to her and to revise later. He taught her that literary art resulted from an organic process in the writer's mind and that one need not follow slavishly any set rules or artificially preconceived plan.

In *A Backward Glance,* she regarded the delay in her artistic maturation as due to the fact that, except for Berry's, she had had no encouragement in her early days. Though he analyzed and criticized, she felt that he had never interfered with the "soul" of her writing. In 1911, she read each evening to him what she had done on *Ethan Frome* that morning; and they paid close attention to the accuracy of background. When they were separated by the demands of his judgeship, she mailed manuscripts to him which he carefully emended and returned with letters of criticism. She recalls that he continued these painstaking efforts in her behalf even when he was seriously ill for months at a time. In ill health after World War I, he continued to revise her work, including *The Age of Innocence,* as she completed each chapter. One can hardly overestimate the influence of his meticulous criticism since it pervaded her books over a thirty-year span.

Upon Berry's death in 1927, she inherited his books, many of which they had read together. She immediately recovered those of her letters that he had saved over their long years of friendship and burned them. In a funeral procession of much pomp and splendor, high French officials followed Berry's coffin drawn by four horses through the streets of Paris to the cathedral. Some two weeks later the burial of his ashes was to be made in Edith Wharton's garden at Pavillon Colombe, where she had erected an altar for the requiem mass. Disagreement among his relatives caused the burial to be made in the Cimetière des Gonards, Versailles, where the graves of Edith Wharton and Walter Berry adjoin each other. For the day of his burial, her diary reads: "The stone closed over all my life."

Though many have found the treatment of her love for Berry too reticent in *A Backward Glance,* her feeling, nevertheless, emerges eloquently in this tribute: "I cannot picture what the life of the spirit would have been to me without him. He found me when my mind and soul were hungry and thirsty, and he fed them till our last hour together" (119).

III   *Morton Fullerton: "a touch of wings brushing by"*

In the latter part of Edith Wharton's marriage, from 1908 to 1910, she fell in love with another man, Morton Fullerton, an American journalist stationed in the Paris office of the *London Times* who had visited the Whartons at Lenox in autumn of 1907.[2] Because a more intense physical attraction existed in her feelings for him than for either Teddy Wharton or Walter Berry, the affair held for her ecstasy and also poignant suffering and frustration. Prior to the account of this affair revealed in the definitive biography by R. W. B. Lewis, a few excerpts from the diary that she devoted to the relationship with Fullerton were prematurely printed. Because these were generally thought to refer to Walter Berry, many have assumed that her friendship with Berry had become adultery several years prior to her divorce.

In the diary, she reveals that the relationship with Fullerton was bewildering. When he angers her, she finds her love increases. Her sense of humiliation emerges when she acknowledges that emotion has destroyed her pride and independent identity. Several entries express her frustrated wish for their meetings to be in secluded and romantic settings and for the sexual experience to merge with an intellectual and spiritual communion. Certainly one of the ironies of

Edith Wharton's life lies in that her associations with several men — her husband, Walter Berry, Henry James, and Fullerton — offered significant companionship, but all were limited. Like many female characters in her novels and stories, she never found in one man the love that included physical, mental, and esthetic elements. The diary implies always her realization that the Fullerton affair is inevitably evanescent. She longs to be to him "like a touch of wings brushing by you in the darkness, or like the scent of an invisible garden that one passes by on an unknown road."[3]

Morton Fullerton had already engaged in a series of alliances with both men and women. The months of his involvement with Edith Wharton ironically correspond exactly to the period of his engagement to Katherine Fullerton, his cousin who had grown up with the understanding that she was his sister and who had loved him since early childhood. In 1903 she learned that she was not his sister, and they became engaged in October, 1907. In 1910 Katherine married Gordon Gerould and, as Katherine Fullerton Gerould, published fiction with help from Edith Wharton and later wrote admiring criticism of her fiction. Between 1904 and 1909, Fullerton was blackmailed by Henrietta Mirecourt, for whom he had long provided an apartment and who was his mistress during the entire period of his marriage (1903 - 04) to the mother of his daughter. By 1909 Mirecourt had possession of letters to Fullerton implicating at least two famous people, if not Edith Wharton: Ronald Gower, a homosexual sculptor and friend of Oscar Wilde, and Margaret Brooke, Ranee of Sarawak, who had borne seven royal children for the white Rajah before returning from Africa with her three surviving sons and becoming involved with Fullerton. The Ranee's letters, like Edith Wharton's diary, suggest her fear that, as a middle-aged woman of propriety and high social position, she has made herself appear foolish. In 1909 Edith Wharton conspired with Henry James to pay the blackmailer and retrieve the incriminating letters. To avoid a bank record indicating transfer of her funds to Fullerton, she paid James, who in turn paid Fullerton's publisher, who in turn gave an advance on royalties for a book that Fullerton never produced.

The emotional upheaval of the affair with Fullerton must have extended her ability to understand and depict the passion and frustration of Anna Leath in *The Reef* (1912). After a quiet marriage, Anna finds herself as a middle-aged widow overwhelmed by her response

to a lover whom she cannot admire. In the perspective of Edith
Wharton's long career, her interest in Fullerton seems less central
than does her affection for Walter Berry and their long comradeship.

IV Divorce and Expatriation

Beginning in the spring of 1908, Teddy Wharton had numerous
affairs and spent Edith's money irresponsibly. The deterioration of
the Whartons' marriage was concurrent with her liaison with Fullerton, with her rise to fame after the publication of *The House of
Mirth* (1905), with her developing friendship with Henry James, and
with her absorption in her art. Though she was now finding a life of
her own in which her husband had little part, the precipitating cause
of the divorce must surely have been the worsening mental illness of
Teddy Wharton.

In the winter of 1903 - 1904, when James called on her in London
for the first time, Edward was depressed for four months. Edith
wrote anxiously in 1909 of her husband's headaches and malaise and
also mentioned two earlier breakdowns. By this time, she knew that
he had appropriated a large amount of her money to support his sexual and social life. In 1910 he entered a sanatorium, but in 1911 he
had apparently recovered to the point that few people could suspect
illness.

But her situation worsened. One sign of Edward Wharton's instability was his determination to control the couple's money and
property. His relatives refused to acknowledge the seriousness of his
illness and prevented Edith from arranging long-term treatment for
him or from assuming control of the trust fund she had inherited.
Earlier, she had been glad for Teddy to manage all her finances.
Erratically now, he resisted her attempts to manage the house at
Lenox with its staff of twenty and to administer her royalties. By
1910 every physician confirmed the diagnosis that Teddy could not
recover; and she decided to sell The Mount and to live in France.
She became an expatriate, despite James's frequent warnings that
his own expatriation had not been satisfactory for him as an
American writer. After her divorce from Edward in 1913, she
returned to America for only one visit when, in 1923, she became the
first woman to receive an honorary doctorate from Yale University.

In 1928, the year after Berry's death, Edward died in Lenox at the
age of seventy-eight. His will mentioned only his nurse. Following
his death, Edith Wharton wrote an old friend thanking her for
remembering Teddy when he had been "a charming companion and

the kindest and most sympathetic of beings" and regretting the ignorance that existed about mental illness. She recalled the physician who had assured the Whartons before Teddy's marriage to her that he could not inherit his father's insanity. In *A Backward Glance,* she writes compassionately of his slow surrender to madness, acknowledging the reluctant death of her affectionate concern, if not passionate love, for him: "His sweetness of temper and boyish enjoyment of life struggled long against the creeping darkness" (326).

V   *The Early Literary Career (1893 - 1914)*

While Edith Wharton's career as a significant novelist begins with *The House of Mirth* (1905), she had already achieved recognition for her short stories. Reviewers labelled them Jamesian because of their epigrammatic quality and stylized dialogue. They are more direct than James's stories, however, and they develop a dramatically compressed situation rather than a meticulously elaborated one. *The Greater Inclination* (1899), *Crucial Instances* (1902), and *The Descent of Man* (1904) contain twenty-four stories, but another eight or ten in magazines were not collected.

In this period, her non-fiction reveals her sophistication as a scholar, her versatility, and her love of art, history, and nature. The printed copies of the first edition of *The Decoration of Houses* (1897) were exhausted immediately, as was the English edition. In *Italian Villas and Their Gardens* (1904) she concentrated on plantings rather than houses, providing descriptive notes for the famous gardens in Maxfield Parrish's illustrations. She also included details about the dimensions of shrubs and flower beds and about the effects to be achieved by variations in levels, patterns of shade and light, and curves. The book became at once a manual for architects and landscape gardeners, and she regretted that the publishers had not allowed her to include scale drawings for the houses and the gardens. While she had been working on *Italian Villas,* she had observed the impressive monuments that she was to describe in such loving detail in *Italian Backgrounds* (1905). In both works she anticipates the informal, colloquial quality of all her travel books, despite her habitual use of scholarly detail and historical allusion.

Her early novellas, *The Touchstone* (1901) and *Sanctuary* (1903), are apprentice-work; and they show less sophistication and control than her short stories. In *The Touchstone,* the protagonist experiences guilt after he sells at great profit the love letters that a famous novelist, Margaret Aubyn, had written to him. Of most in-

terest is the polished, epigrammatic style characteristic of the early
fiction and the stylized dialogue which Wharton substitutes for conversation. The sentences are brilliant but tend to be separable from
their context and to call attention to themselves as the terse
statements in her best work seldom do: "One felt that if she had
been prettier, she would have had emotions instead of ideas." "He
liked the collective point of view that goes with the civilized unifor-
mity of dress-clothes."

Sanctuary (1903) presents a more believable sinner, Denis Payton,
who suffers less from his guilt than he should after defrauding his
sister-in-law and causing her suicide and the death of her child. His
fiancée, Kate Orme, provides the "intelligence" through whom the
tense situation between them slowly develops. Kate's recognition of
his perfidy builds incrementally, as does her decision to marry him
though she now despises him. Since she knows his obloquy, she feels
that only she is qualified to counteract her husband's influence over
any child of his. She decides, in short, to be a martyr for the sake of
hypothetical children. In the second section, Mrs. Wharton exhaustively analyzes Kate's consciousness as she — having long been
a widow — waits to see whether her now grown son will resist the
temptation to appropriate a dead friend's architectural designs.
Although his fiancée urges him to do so, he rises superior to the
temptation. Kate thus succeeds in her mission — to provide Payton's
offspring with a moral force that compensates for any inherited
weakness.

Edith Wharton's first novel, the two-volume Valley of Decision
(1902), centers on the conflict between an individual's need for
freedom and his inevitable loss of some of that freedom in an
ordered society — one of her recurrent themes. She called the book
"not . . . a novel at all, but only a romantic chronicle" (205). This
chronicle, laid in eighteenth-century Italy, first presents the
development of Odo Valsecca from childhood among the peasants
through his adolescence and the loss of religious conviction as a
result of his learning. His study of philosophy causes him to embrace
for a time the political and metaphysical ideas that brought about
the French Revolution. To finance reforms in his duchy when he
comes to power, he marries the rich widow of another duke and
makes Fulvia, who is the woman he loves and the daughter of his
professor, his mistress. After a mob kills her, supposedly as a witch,
Odo becomes increasingly reactionary and eventually opposes
political change of any kind. In the end, the revolutionaries, whom

he had helped, overthrow him as a tyrant intent on preserving the old order.

Edith Wharton's love for the Italian landscape and her immersion in eighteen-century Italy are evident throughout this novel, especially in the vivid details which are assimilated in the action and the characters. Her extensive research included such projects as making lists of the perfumes that a duchess might have used and of the most popular lap dogs among Italian gentry. Odo's reactions to specific philosophical theories and to art history as he studies with his professor undoubtedly reflect Edith Wharton's own enthusiasms. Perhaps Odo's wistful skepticism when he goes to mass in the cold dawn in order to recapture a lost religious fervor reflects her own incertitude as a young woman.

Reaction to the novel was mixed. Theodore Roosevelt never forgave his friend for failing to have Odo marry Fulvia. Agnes Repplier, who typified the "genteel" aversion which many of Edith Wharton's early critics felt toward her sexual frankness and religious skepticism, declared that "no refined woman would be willing to associate her name even with the condemnation of it." Generally, however, the reception was enthusiastic. Reviews described it as "a classic," as "giantlike," and as "the most splendid achievement of any American man or woman in fiction." Charles Eliot Norton, who had helped her in her research, wrote to a colleague that her book was "a unique and astonishing performance," and years later Van Wyck Brooks declared that "in power of imagination few novels have . . . surpassed it." This estimate is excessive; for, though the book is brilliant in places and its characters have life, Mrs. Wharton was not yet able to sustain imaginatively a book of this length. In none of her later fiction did she again reach farther into history than her parents' generation.

Edith Wharton's first five novels established her place in American letters and illustrate her versatility. The massive *Valley of Decision* was followed by *The House of Mirth* (1905). Its appealing, complex, and pathetic heroine, Lily Bart, exerted a universal appeal to novel readers and critics alike. Within two months, this novel broke records for sales, and Edith Wharton, previously known for her short stories, became a celebrity. *The House of Mirth*, an outstanding novel of manners, marked the emergence of a major literary artist. Her literary career was assured.

Other major works, novels and novellas, followed. *The Fruit of the Tree* (1907), though less firmly controlled than *The House of Mirth*,

illustrates the breadth of Edith Wharton's interests through her absorption in marital incompatibility, factory reform, insurance fraud,
and the autocratic power that physicians exercise over nurses. A
novella, *Madame de Treymes* (1907), generated favorable attention
because of its Jamesian concentration on a single situation and
because of the meticulously observed reactions of a few individuals
to that situation. Another novella, *Ethan Frome* (1911), with its incisive irony and its bleak landscape used to heighten human suffering, was no great commercial or critical success. But its popularity
with the reading public increased until by 1920 it had become the
best-known of Edith Wharton's works, and it remains the book with
which the average reader associates her. She herself felt that the
public had not only fastened too tenaciously upon *Ethan Frome* as
her most representative work but also tended to overlook her other
important books.

One of her more complicated and carefully wrought novels, *The
Reef*, appeared in 1912. In it, she concentrated, with Jamesian
firmness, upon four characters and the intensification of their
emotional relationships to one another, much as if she had had
James's *The Golden Bowl* in her consciousness as she wrote her
novel. The specialized subject and decor of *The Reef* and its virtuosity limited its general appeal; and the critics tended to be more
respectful than enthusiastic. Nevertheless, its solidity of construction
and its acuteness of insight place it just below her very best novels.

With *The Custom of the Country* (1913) Edith Wharton again
wrote a major novel, which represents — along with *The House of
Mirth* and *The Age of Innocence* — the pinnacle of her achievement. Where *The House of Mirth* had been compassionate in its
drift, this novel was sardonic in tone and satiric in emphasis. The
novel spreads widely from a primitive Midwest America to the
elegant New York social scene to the culture and civilization of
France. Its canvas is wide, and Mrs. Wharton's powers of social
observation were never more discerning. It is the most massive of her
novels, although it is more abrasive than *The House of Mirth* and
The Age of Innocence and a less engaging work. Its main characters
are satirically, rather than sympathetically, conceived. But the esthetic control that it reveals, its sustained vitality, and its psychological penetration combine to establish it as one of her masterpieces.

In view of the fact that Edith Wharton wrote little before forty
and then only gradually regarded herself as a professional, the

magnitude and versatility of her achievement in the dozen years preceding World War I are extraordinary. Had her canon included only the works produced in these years, she would still be regarded as a distinguished American artist. By 1913 she had published six collections of short stories, a book of poems, a translated play, numerous critical articles, and books on interior decorating, Italian gardens, Italian architecture, and travel in France. She had written four novellas and five full-length novels. Altogether, she had, before the war, established herself as a prolific writer, a meticulous and versatile craftsman, a careful recorder of manners, and a woman possessing broad social concern.

VI *Friendship with Henry James (1903 - 1916)*

When the Whartons attended a dinner party with Henry James in the late 1880's and another in Venice in 1890, Edith lacked the courage to converse with him. Mutual friends (Paul Bourget, Mary Cadwaladar Jones, and Howard Sturgis, in particular) had prepared the way for the two authors to meet. In 1889 James wrote the Bourgets that Edith Wharton's best stories in *The Greater Inclination* revealed her own self, while the other stories showed another person. One may assume that the other person was James himself, whose influence he saw excessively reflected in them, because he then expressed a wish to visit with this woman who seemed too susceptible.

He did not write her, however, until almost a year later — after he had encountered another story, "The Line of Least Resistance," and had found it brilliant. In his first letter (October 26, 1900) he urged her to continue her study of *American* life. Having read *Crucial Instances, The Touchstone,* and *The Valley of Decision,* James confided to Mrs. Jones in 1902 that he liked her sister-in-law's "diabolical little cleverness, the . . . intelligence in her style, and her sharp eye for an interesting *kind* of subject."[5]

In December, 1903, when James called on Edith Wharton in London, he was over sixty and she over forty. She was in the "first fever" of her writing, while he had a long career behind him. His reputation as a writer noted for an involuted, subtle, oblique style was confirmed with the appearance of *The Wings of Dove* (1902), *The Ambassadors* (1903), and *The Golden Bowl* (1904). At the beginning of their friendship he was best known for his less involuted novels such as *The American* (1877), *Daisy Miller* (1879), and *The Portrait of a Lady* (1881). Just before he visited America in 1904 (for the first time since 1883), he had read *The Descent of Man*, Edith Wharton's third collection of short stories; and he wrote her that he liked its wise and witty art.

During his American visit, James stayed with the Whartons at Lenox in the autumn of 1904, visited a few days in their New York apartment at Christmas, again went to Lenox in the summer of 1905, and, in general, consolidated his friendship with them. Writing from Lenox to Howard Sturgis in the fall of 1904, he described The Mount as "a delicate French château mirrored in a Massachusetts pond" and as a reflection of "the almost too impeccable taste of its so accomplished mistress." Because his host and hostess were kindness and hospitality incarnate, James confided whimsically, "you needn't bring supplementary apples or candies in your dressing bag."[6] In all the years of their friendship James remained conscious of his more limited means, remarking once that the usual income among the Whartons' friends seemed to be a million a year.

Although he commented that New England was building too many roads, he, like Edith Wharton, became enthusiastic about touring. He drove every afternoon with the Whartons. Teddy sat in front with the chauffeur. Besides the long drives, there were the mornings when they wrote undisturbed and then evenings of talk in which Teddy figured little. James referred to the couple as the "Edith Whartons" and mentioned that Teddy was "sandwiched between" them (Edel, 262). Edith Wharton recalls one evening when James read Walt Whitman, a lifelong favorite of hers, in a crooning tone, "his voice filling the room like an organ adagio," and then they talked of the poet, "tossing back and forth to each other treasure after treasure" (186).

In 1907, James, who had not been to the Continent for eight years, spent two weeks in the Whartons' Paris apartment which he later called the House of Mirth. In half-grudging, half-pleased acceptance of their hospitality, he refers in letters at this point to "pampered Princesses," to the woman's energy "devouring and desolating, ravaging, burning, and destroying;" and to "the rich, rushing, ravening Whartons" (Edel, 340). He later went with them through Southern France, a journey that Edith Wharton reported in *A Motor-Flight Through France* (1908).

James and Berry had become friends at The Mount. After his return to England, James wrote to Edith Wharton mentioning Berry as the man who had greatly endeared himself to him. He saw him as one gifted and unhappy. Gradually, he came to understand the

Whartons' strained marital situation and included in his letters such comments as, "I hope you've not wanted for the sight of Walter Berry" (Edel, 257). Though he found Edith somewhat dictatorial, with energy that exhausted him, he also found her dramatic and fascinating, and he was humorous in his complaints.

Edith Wharton believed that James had not made money commensurate with his fame. She resorted once to an ingenious plot to get eight thousand dollars of her royalties transferred to his account at Scribner's so that he could be paid a large advance on a book; and while James's agent learned of the transfer, James never did. She was unsuccessful, however, even with the help of William Dean Howells, in getting the Nobel Prize for him, and she failed notoriously in her third scheme — to raise funds for a gift on his seventieth birthday in 1912. When James's nephew advised him of the solicitation, James denounced it as reckless and indiscreet, though he may never have mentioned the subject to her.

Poignant are the letters in which James offered support to her as he endured his final illness. But greater than their support of each other in adversity was their ability to laugh at identical things. They had, Edith Wharton remarked, a sense of "irony pitched in exactly the same key" (173). His "elaborate hesitancies," which were so annoying to many, were to her "a cobweb bridge . . . an invisible passage over which one knew that silver-footed ironies, veiled jokes, tiptoe malices were stealing to explode a huge laugh at one's feet" (178).

Even before she had met Henry James, reviewers generally identified her work with his. Certainly she followed James in a concern with technique, in a conviction that the formal properties of writing are important, and in a conscious experimentation within the tenets she had established for herself as esthetician and writer. But whether she can be designated a disciple who learned her technique through conversation with the "master" is doubtful, for tentativeness characterized both authors in their reluctance to give advice or to follow it. Both searched for the characteristics of good fiction in the work of great masters, and both tried to gain from such study a knowledge of the craft of fiction.

James and Edith Wharton were convinced that discussion of theory was positive in its effects upon artists. At all times in her long career she followed James's conviction, expressed in "The Art of Fiction," about the importance of literary theory. As James stated, "Art lives upon discussion, upon experiment, upon curiosity, upon variety of attempt, upon the exchange of views and the comparison of stand-points. . . . The successful application of any art is a delightful spec-tacle, but the theory too is interesting. . . . Discussion, suggestion, formulation, these things are fertilizing."

Many authors, Mrs. Wharton knew, feared that the analysis of their creative processes, the formulation of principles governing technique, or even the close study of fiction written by others might interfere with their own creativity. She admitted in *The Writing of Fiction* (1925) that some writers, including James, became ex-cessively preoccupied in their search for new forms and for complex effects. But such writers, she saw, might be esthetic pioneers and build "intellectual houses for the next generation to live in" (117) even when they could not realize in their own work the possibilities suggested by their theories.

Both James and Wharton knew that they must search for valid generalizations about writing, but both knew also that following such precepts did not in itself insure memorable work. Edith Whar-ton expressed in *The Writing of Fiction* her conviction that a writer is obliged to speculate about his craft even though his inspiration can never be rationally defined: "if no art can be quite pent-up in the rules deduced from it, neither can it fully realize itself unless those who practice it attempt to take its measure and reason out its processes" (119).

She resented the popular view that her work was derivative from James and that she was his subservient disciple. He evidently felt frustration in attempting to be her mentor, not merely because he understood her imaginative independence and energetic confidence, but because (as he confessed in 1902) he could never properly suggest specific changes in any finished work. He always had to go back to the initial kernel of a story and let it grow in his mind to see how it should go; then the story would become his own — a new work of fiction, not that of the author he wished to help.

When James did scrutinize her work, he showed little tact, but she suggests that he was clumsy and honest rather than unkind or malicious. In *A Backward Glance* she recounts several incidents such as the one in which, after praising *The Custom of the Country*, he commented, "but of course you know — as how should you, with your infernal keenness of perception, *not* know — that in doing your tale you had under your hand a magnificent subject, which ought to have been your main theme, and that you used it as mere incident and then passed it by" (182).

When *The Fruit of the Tree* (1907) was published, a Marxist paper asked James to review it and implied that Edith had suggested his name. When she denied this allegation, James remarked that perhaps he might "really dedicate a few lucid remarks to the mystery of your genius." But, upon reading her book, he disliked the "strangely infirm" construction, and he simply told her she had employed "more *kinds* of interest than anyone now going can pretend to achieve." Leon Edel notes that, in James's parody of this novel in "The Velvet Glove," originally entitled "The Top of the Tree," he has Amy Evans overuse the word *all:* "all the Amy Evans in her," "all the conscious conqueror in him," and "all the conscientious man of letters in him" (Edel, 352 - 59). *The Fruit of the Tree* had contained many phrases like "all the ardor" and "all the warm instincts."

Like James's comments about Wharton's work, her criticism of his could be unintentionally deflating. Assuming he had used a deliberate system of characterization in *The Golden Bowl* and anxious to hear his reasons for employing it, she asked: "What was your idea in suspending the four principal characters . . . in the void? What sort of life did they lead when they were not watching each other? Why have you stripped them of all the *human fringes* we necessarily trail after us through life?" She was sorry that she had spoken when he responded with pained surprise, "My dear — I didn't know I had" (191).

James produced the prefaces to the New York edition of his work during these years of friendship with Edith Wharton. Clearly evident in them are similarities not only between the pronouncements he makes and her statements but, more important, perhaps, between their main subjects of criticism and fiction.[7] For instance, James uses as pervasive themes the relationship between art and life, the relationship between the artist and his art, and the relationship between the artist and his life. With Mrs. Wharton, exploration of these themes dominates her early stories: in *Crucial Instances* five of her seven stories center on artists. Outlines, abortive versions, and letters to her publishers indicate that for thirty years she planned the writing of *Literature,* a novel which would trace the growth of an artist. From these false starts grew *Hudson River Bracketed* (1929) and *The Gods Arrive* (1932). In these books Vance Weston, using for his work his own suffering and his own life, develops into a successful novelist and a perceptive human being who can reach beyond preoccupation with self.

Both James and Wharton employed international themes. In her work the European characters — except for Raymond de Chelle in *The Custom of the Country*, a few characters in *The Buccaneers*, and Madame de Treymes — are undeveloped or used as background figures. The chief characters remain American, though displaced. In her fiction the effect of Europe on the individual is generally of less consequence than in James.

Moreover, both explored extensively the supernatural, although Mrs. Wharton confined her use of it to the short story. Like James, she concentrates not only on the supernatural phenomenon but on its effect upon one who observes it. In their ghost tales, both authors seek symbolic and moral interpretations, rather than chilling sensations alone. Both also frequently used the influence of the dead over the living. Such rationally demonstrated influence of dead people, quite apart from the use of ghosts, appears in Mrs. Wharton's work even before her friendship with James. For instance, even in her first novella, the dead dominate the living. In *The Touchstone*, the dead novelist, whose letters the protagonist sold, influences from her grave the lives of all the characters. In *Sanctuary* the unseen presence of the drowned woman and her child, who were defrauded by Payton, produce Kate Orme's contempt for her fiancée. In the second part of the book, the felt presence of the now dead Payton, whose son may inherit his weakness of moral fibre, intensifies Kate's anguish as she watches the son struggle against temptation. In *The Fruit of the Tree* (1907) Bessie, innocuous in her lifetime, after her death becomes in her husband's eyes a woman of heroic proportions; and, for him, his second wife fades into insignificance.

In matters related to craft, marked resemblances exist between James's views and Edith Wharton's. Both saw the potentialities of the novella for developing situations beyond the limits permitted in the short-story form. Edith Wharton's work includes eleven novellas, three written before she knew James. Like him, she intellectualized her fiction, making minimal use of the dramatic scene directly presented to the reader; she emphasized instead an expository approach. Scenes are saved for culminating moments. Her first collection of stories, *Crucial Instances*, illustrates even in its title the principle that she held in common with James — each scene must suggest larger patterns of experience.

A central intelligence, capable of making fine distinctions, ordinarily views the action in the works of both authors and relates the individual scene to a larger context. In a third of Wharton's stories a narrator provides this consciousness. She had, in fact, perfected her use of the crucial instance, reflected through a central consciousness, long before she wrote *Ethan Frome* (1911). In this masterful example of the technique, her vivid details and dramatic scenes become important not in themselves but for whatever they reveal to the central intelligence. We are only incidentally conscious of Edith Wharton as a Realist who documents her narrative by presenting Ethan's fate as a vision in the mind of the engineer who serves as narrator. Similarly, in *The Reef* (1912), a series of crucial instances reveals a larger pattern; but what is impressive is not the situation so much as the effects on the sensibilities of the "fine central intelligence," the passionate and inhibited Anna Leath. Simple difficulties occurring in the "crucial" scenes intensify and become overwhelming dramatic problems for Anna Leath through whom the reader's apprehension of these scenes must come. Significantly, James highly praised both *Ethan Frome* and *The Reef*.

In their efforts to attain economy, both James and Wharton advocated a sparse use of dialogue. Expository interpretation by a central consciousness moves a story along faster in one paragraph than several pages of dialogue which might later need interpretation. The novelist, Edith Wharton contended, possesses freedom beyond the dramatist who must express everything in speech. Dialogue in Wharton and James tends to be a stylized suggestion of conversation, but Wharton's mannered interchanges become more colloquial later in her career. She maintained, as did James, that dialogue should be reserved for crucial scenes. The intervening narrative produces the illusion of passing time; dialogue enhances the impression that time has indeed passed when the scene in which it occurs comes to an end. Both authors stressed the need to "foreshorten time" and the difficulty of so doing. Edith Wharton, in fact, considered it a problem so complicated that few writers have solved it. Their secret remains "the great mystery of the art of fiction," an incommunicable experience that comes through the novelist's living with his characters through a significant period of time.

The two writers were fastidious about style, and they were careful about the structure of their narratives. Mrs. Wharton develops her views relative to this aspect of her craft in *The Writing of Fiction*. Both writers, moreover, experimented continually with the various uses of irony; in the work of both, irony deepened and mellowed with their increased maturity and understanding of human nature.

Mrs. Wharton remarked in *A Backward Glance* that she had known

only two writers deeply interested in technique — Paul Bourget and
James, that she had talked frequently with both, but that, about certain points, she had always disagreed with them. James and Mrs.
Wharton developed the narrative artistry from similar presup-
positions, but she exemplified them less consistently. As far as
James's own work was concerned, she disapproved of the involuted
prose in his later work, and she thought he sometimes saw his
characters only in relation to each other, not in a larger context.
While he stressed a predesigned structure, she tended more and
more to work without one, declaring in 1934 that "design, in his
strict geometrical sense, is to me one of the least important things in
fiction" (190).
     Ultimately this friendship is more significant on personal terms
than intellectual ones. She reveals her great admiration in her asser-
tion at his death that those who knew him well knew "how great he
would have been if he had never written a line" (Edel, 560). James
might have enjoyed equally his friendship for Edith Wharton if she
had never written a line, even though they explored so eagerly with
each other the rationale of their narrative art. They were friends who
supported each other, they enjoyed each other's company, they
respected each other's work, and they enlarged each other's conceptions of narrative art. As James lay dying, Edith Wharton wrote:
"His friendship was the pride and honor of my life."[8]

VII   The War Years (1914 - 1918)

     A second stage of Edith Wharton's life and career began after her
sale of The Mount in 1911: her expatriation, broken after this date
only by a visit of a few days in 1923 to receive a doctorate from Yale;
her divorce in 1913; and her full-time commitment for four years to
war relief in Paris. When Edith Wharton returned to Paris in 1914,
many Parisians, including the government officials, had moved to
Bordeaux. The Red Cross and government agencies, occupied with
their work at the front, assigned the care of refugees to volunteers
behind the lines. Charles Du Bos, who had ten years before
translated the French edition of The House of Mirth, organized a
relief project, first called the Accueil Franco-Belge and later the Accueil Franco-Americain, with Mrs. Wharton as head of the American
committee. Mrs. Royall Tyler, Mary Cadwaladar Jones, and Anna
Bahlmann (Edith Wharton's governess who by 1900 had become her
secretary) served as her chief aides.
     In offices near the Champs-Elysees, from nine in the morning to

midnight, the volunteers distributed meal tickets, clothing, and information about lodging. The organization comprised ten units: a workroom for needlewomen, an employment agency, a furniture store, a restaurant, bread and grocery distribution centers, hospital rooms, a dental clinic, an isolation ward, and several tuberculosis sanatoriums.[9] In 1918 the *Accueil* was caring for five thousand refugees resettled in Paris, it had established four colonies for old people and children in rural areas near the city, and it had acquired four sanatoriums for women and children with tuberculosis. During the war the personnel at the center lodged thirty thousand refugees, found work for eight thousand, and treated one hundred thousand military personnel ill with tuberculosis. When the Queen of Belgium appealed to Mrs. Wharton on behalf of six hundred and fifty orphans, aged one to fifteen, Mrs. Wharton established the Children of Flanders Rescue Committee to care for displaced children and to send them to French families who lived farthest from the battle zones. She even cared for six children in her own apartment and, after the war, found homes for each and sent money to their foster parents.

Fighting France (1914) contrasts ironically with her earlier travel book, *A Motor-Flight through France* (1908). With the 1914 book, which describes a journey taken under authorization of the military to inspect hospitals in battle areas, Edith Wharton aimed to hasten American entry into the war. The trip provided the milieu for *A Son at the Front* (1922) in which the hero's parents get permission to search for their wounded son and then to stay for several days in his field hospital. *In Morocco* records Mrs. Wharton's journey in 1917 to Africa as the honored guest of the French government. For her war activities, France also decorated her in 1917 with the Cross of the Legion of Honor, rarely awarded to women. In *The Marne* (1918), a novella about a young American who fights for France, Mrs. Wharton surprisingly fuses a precise, documentary treatment of battle with a ghost-story ending.

In addition to daily work at the center, Mrs. Wharton wrote letters at night to raise funds, and she attempted to make each letter a personal one. In *The Book of the Homeless* (1916) she compiled works which writers, musicians, and artists donated for the cause. Igor Stravinsky provided a musical score; Max Beerbohm, Claude Monet, Jean Renoir, and Auguste Rodin gave illustrations and paintings; and Joseph Conrad, John Galsworthy, Thomas Hardy, William Dean Howells, Henry James, George Santayana, and William Butler Yeats contributed essays, poems, and fiction; Sarah Bernhardt and Eleanora Duse furnished letters. Theodore Roosevelt wrote the introduction, and Mrs. Wharton translated all the materials not written in English. Besides her war-related books, she published in 1917 *Summer* and *Xingu and Other Stories,* which contained "Bunner Sisters" written in the 1890's. This long story, like *Ethan Frome* and *Summer,* dealt with the frustrated rebellion of the poor and their enforced stoicism.

VIII   The Late Years (1918 - 1937)

After the war Edith Wharton continued her expatriate existence. Her notable contacts with America came through her large correspondence and her visit to America for a few days in 1923 when she became the first woman to receive an honorary doctorate from Yale University. She became the first woman Gold Medallist of the American Society of Arts and Letters in 1924. In 1918 she began remodelling the eighteenth-century Pavillon Calombe and in 1920 moved to the country after more than ten years in the Rue de Varenne. By 1920 she was also restoring an ancient monastery at Hyéris, where she spent her winters for the rest of her life. Edith Wharton, now fifty-six, knew that she had overtaxed herself for four years with the rigorous activities and anxiety occasioned by the war. Her physician remarked that her health was precarious and that she was "an elastic stretched too far, that will never tighten up again."[10] She lacked at that time the detachment to write *A Son at the Front.* Accordingly, it did not appear until two years after the success of *The Age of Innocence* (1920), in which she looked back, both nostalgically and cynically, to her parents' generation. She returned to this same period in *Old New York* (1924).

The Age of Innocence vies with *The House of Mirth* and *The Custom of the Country* for the honor of being Mrs. Wharton's masterpiece. It is her most seasoned and, artistically, her most fully-wrought book. Again she registered, as in her other first-rank books, the interplay of her figures with the society that produced them and with which they had come to terms. Having mellowed since *The Custom of the Country,* she wrote a compassionate as well as satiric account of life in old New York in *The Age of Innocence.*

In 1921 she received the Pulitzer Prize for this novel, though two members of the committee, Stuart P. Sherman and Robert Morss Lovett, announced publicly that they had wanted the prize to go to Sinclair Lewis for *Main Street.* They emphasized the nostalgic aspect of the book, the presence of which no reader would deny, but they failed to recognize that Mrs. Wharton was critical rather than sentimental in her presentation of this past. In *Hudson River Bracketed* she recounts the awarding of a Pulsifer Prize, an indication perhaps that she took the honor lightly and disliked the imputation that she had received the prize by default. That this novel does achieve a universal dimension most appreciative readers have since recognized. It is, at once, a masterful evocation of a milieu and a masterful delineation of human beings caught between renunciation and passion.

Two inconsequential books, *The Glimpses of the Moon* (1922) and *The Mother's Recompense* (1925), both serials for *The Pictorial Review*, damaged her reputation. The first novel features hypocritical characters whose significance Edith Wharton did not clearly see. It is a dull tale of a parasitic couple who live in a mansion while the owners are away in return for helping the absent hostess hide her adultery. Mrs. Wharton does manage in the other novel to create a believable character, Kate Cleophane, a divorcée who left America years before in disgrace after she had joined her lover. But the situation in which she finds herself on her return is not credible. Her daughter has taken a lover quite matter-of-factly, and society now seems to accept such irregular liaisons. In the end, Kate lacks the courage — or the cruelty — to tell her daughter that she herself had been the mistress of her daughter's lover. Where Edith Wharton stands concerning the mother's decision is unclear; perhaps Edith Wharton did not know where she herself stood.

Though a better book than these two novels, *A Son at the Front* (1923) gained few partisans. In it Mrs. Wharton failed to achieve full control because she had been so intensely involved in the war and because her sympathies had been so strongly French. Her attempt to gain objectivity by waiting four years to finish the book probably kept it from being the popular success it might have been. Some fine satiric touches in it, directed at those who enjoyed the excitement in the war from behind the lines, foreshadow the explicit satire in her later novels. In *Old New York* (1924) — a quartet of masterful novellas — Edith Wharton returned to the generation of her parents.

She wrote to Margaret Chanler in 1925 confessing how deeply disturbed she had become by adverse reviews of her work. She apologized as a "priestess of the life of reason" for taking her reviews so much to heart but she was perplexed: "As my work reaches its close, I feel so sure that it is either nothing or far more than they know. And I wonder a little desolately which." If little can be said in defense of *The Glimpses of the Moon* and *The Mother's Recompense*, we need not view them as evidence of a decline in the author's creative power. Among thirty-two books of fiction, it would hardly be possible for them all to be first-class. Some of her books fell short of excellence because of her compulsion to come to terms with a new scene and a new generation of Americans even at the expense of her craft. Nevertheless, in this period her work shows great versatility and a wide range of subjects.

During the years 1920 - 1925, in which the two *Pictorial Review* serials appeared, she published better works: *The Age of Innocence*, the *Old New York* quartet, and *The Writing of Fiction*; and she was to produce before her death five more competent novels. In *Twilight Sleep* (1927) and in *The Children* (1928) she experimented with broad satiric effects and with exaggerated characters — the mode she had used so brilliantly in *The Custom of the Country*. In these novels a world caught up in boredom, easy divorce, and too much money registers with immediacy, and we can grant that she has observed the social scene with precision and insight. Yet she also departs from Realistic criteria, and in doing so, sometimes exaggerates her characters and situations beyond the level of effectiveness. In *Hudson River Bracketed* (1929) and *The Gods Arrive* (1932) she too stridently satirizes Euphoria, a Midwest town; superficial literary cliques in New York and Paris; and ostentatious American tourists.

In these two novels the artist-protagonist, Vance Weston, fails to convince us because Mrs. Wharton conceived the incidents involving him and the people surrounding him too coarsely perhaps for the requirements of her work. But the female creations are incisive: Vance's angry aunt, his naive first wife, his mistress Halo Tarrant, and his blowsy childhood sweetheart, who becomes a tycoon. *The Buccaneers* (1937) promised to be among her best novels, had it been finished. In her last fifteen years she also produced some of her finest short stories: "Bewitched," "A Bottle of Perrier," "After Holbein," "Her Son," "The Day of the Funeral," "Pomegranate Seed," "Roman Fever," and "All Souls."

CHAPTER 2

"Sharpening of the Moral Vision": The House of Mirth

*T*HE House of Mirth,[1] Edith Wharton's first widely read novel, marked a turning point, she said, in her control of her craft because she learned from writing it the importance of systematic daily effort in sustaining the intensity of her imagination. To meet an emergency at Scribner's, she agreed to print five chapters immediately and to supply in installments the rest of the novel within six months. At the age of forty-three, she experienced for the first time the somewhat ambiguous stimulus of writing under pressure of deadlines. As a result of her sustained engagement with this novel, it has a clearer design than anything she had written previously. Not only did she handle expertly the intricacies of an extended narrative, but she also learned how to write with economy and concentration, to focus upon one central character, and to confine herself to a few important themes.

I *"The significance of a frivolous society"*

Edith Wharton in *A Backward Glance* (1934) declared that an author who chooses a trivial subject must relate it to a moral crisis or to some other important aspect of human experience. To illustrate, she alluded to *The House of Mirth* in which the significance of a frivolous society — the "trivial" subject she had chosen — lay in what it destroyed. New York society was nefarious, she perceived, precisely because it debased an individual like Lily Bart. Lily descends from a position of prestige and glamor to anonymity and poverty. Actually, the book gains its significance from the further implication that a human being can find victory through suffering apparent defeat in a society that lacks meaning and direction. At the same time that Lily moves toward tragedy, she moves toward understanding of herself and others and reveals that she is in essence superior to those who had formerly represented to her all the social graces.

Lily's destruction is gradual as she moves downward from one social class to another. Early in the book the staid aristocrats (the Gryces, Penistons, Stepneys, Van Alstynes, and Van Osburghs) accept her and view her as being one of them by birth. But she finds life with these people constricting. Searching for pleasure and a rich husband, she seeks another group, the rich and powerful leaders of high society (the Trenors, the Dorsets, Ned Silverton, and Carrie Fisher), who welcome her because of her youth, beauty, and charm. When she tries to keep up with these wealthy acquaintances by moving from house party to house party, she accumulates gambling and dressmaking debts. Gus Trenor, she naively assumes, has invested a pittance for her which is to pay huge dividends. She later discovers that, in exchange for the money which she assumed to be the return from her investment, he expects her to become his mistress. Once Aunt Julia Peniston learns of Lily's debts, she disowns her. Later, when the jealous Bertha Dorset publicly implies that Lily is an adulteress, she becomes a liability rather than an asset to any hostess.

Shunned by her aristocratic relatives and by the *haute monde*, Lily is forced to seek solace and material support from still another group, the nouveau riche (the Brys, the Gormers, and Simon Rosedale). She even thinks of marriage to the vulgar millionaire, Rosedale; but the newly rich lose interest in her when they realize that she can no longer secure for them an entrée into high society. She is forced to earn her living by work which she finds uncongenial. At first, she is a secretary to a divorcée of dubious repute until Lawrence Selden, an idealistic young aristocrat to whom she is attracted, expresses his disapproval. She then tries to become a seamstress in a millinery workshop but lacks adequate training and physical endurance to keep her job. She descends in the social scale until, shortly before her death, she finds refuge in the slum kitchen of Nettie Struther, a prostitute to whom she had once given money. Unemployed and ill, she makes a last visit to Selden, who, despite his idealistic talk of a "republic of the spirit," reflects the obtuseness of a society that overvalues conventions and money. Finally, alone in her room, she is exhausted but victorious over the temptation to blackmail Bertha Dorset, the social leader who has slandered her. She uses the small legacy that she has just received from her aunt's estate to pay her debts rather than to buy food and medicine. During the night, she dies.

Lily's gradual destruction by a hostile society balances, and sometimes accentuates, the novel's more affirmative second theme: her growing aspiration to become independent, unselfish, responsive, and responsible. The night of her death she achieves a selfless humanity: she forgoes vengeance upon Bertha Dorset; she expresses her sympathy for Nettie Struther, a former prostitute; she communicates her affection seriously for the first time to the self-centered Selden, who has too hesitantly loved her; and she uses the legacy to reestablish her financial integrity, rather than to sustain her own life.

Ironically, this victory coincides with her harrowing death; she is now unemployed, disgraced, and excluded by the society that had exploited her youth and beauty. Her simultaneous defeat and victory is convincing rather than melodramatic because Mrs. Wharton has developed both themes contrapuntally. Lily's victory over her own triviality unfortunately makes her vulnerable to a society that cannot appreciate her maturing sensibility and her power of discrimination and that can only be controlled by the ruthlessness which Simon Rosedale recommends to Lily.

Though Selden criticizes the moneyed society of which he is a part, he is so much a refined hedonist that he is never able to break away from it. He lacks vigor and stamina; he prefers books and dining with other aristocrats to practicing law with dedication. Early in the book, he tells Lily to leave her vulgar, wealthy friends in order to seek a "republic of the spirit," but he has no notion of the irrelevance of such advice to Lily whose financial situation is precarious. Despite his propriety, which makes him apprehensive about marriage to the slightly unconventional Lily, he has, as the book begins, just finished an affair with Bertha Dorset who now has a new lover, Ned Silverton. At first Lily herself hesitates to marry Selden because she is anxious about his modest means; nevertheless, she belatedly discovers that she loves him. Even later, he recognizes fully his love for her.

Selden's self-righteous remarks about the republic of the spirit somewhat ironically sustain Lily during her last lonely months. On her way to blackmail Bertha Dorset, who has irreparably damaged her reputation, Lily pauses for her last talk with Selden — one that contrasts with their conversation at the opening of the novel, when she is lighthearted and ambitious. She appeals to him to have faith in her and speaks of the insights she has gained through her suffering. The appeal is justified because her courage is great, but Selden can-

not rise to her appeal. She is no longer evasive about important
emotions and relationships; Selden, who had criticized her artifice
and lack of seriousness, now reacts to her directness with embarrassment and constraint. At this crucial moment he affects a light tone to
conceal his awkwardness. The rigid aristocratic world has made him
incapable of sharing in the "republic of the spirit" she offers him,
that same republic that he had so forcefully once recommended to
her.

The sardonic aspect of the novel is even more intense at this moment than it is the next morning after Lily's death when Selden
ironically arrives too late to declare his love. Mrs. Wharton's pity for
Lily on her last visit to Selden balances the ruthlessness of the ex-
posure of Selden in the scene. Lily is no longer the slave of a
worthless society, for she has attained maturity, even serenity, by her
suffering. In contrast, Selden is paralyzed by propriety and by the
debilitating standards of the society that he ostensibly scorns, its
evasiveness, hypocrisy, and intellectual lassitude; and he is unable to
react spontaneously to Lily's "outrush of feeling." She has finally escaped the constricting values of her society; her "liberator" has not.
He is imprisoned in "the house of mirth."

Balancing Lily's defeat, Mrs. Wharton emphasizes "the continuity
of life" which Lily discovers in Nettie Struther's dingy kitchen,
rather than Selden's somewhat abstract "republic of the spirit." Lily
realizes that all the people from the aristocracy and the wealthy
bourgeoisie have nothing to sustain them; they settle for the glittering illusion or for the glamorous appearance; and, as a result, they
seem to be alone even when together — as "atoms whirling away
from each other." Nettie, who has lived as a girl of the streets and
has recently recovered from tuberculosis, and her husband accept
each other for what they are. On this basis of mutual trust, they build
a shelter for themselves and their baby against the harsh world outside, though Lily recognizes how tenuous even such a shelter may
be: "it had the frail, audacious permanence of a bird's nest" (519).

Besides Selden, the other most fully developed characters are Gerty Farish and Simon Rosedale. Though Lily is somewhat contemp-
tuous of them, she also turns to them at times of crisis. Gerty, a social
worker of aristocratic family, is plain and allows herself to be taken
for granted. She has much strength of character and realizes that her
work with the poor provides "that sharpening of the moral vision
which makes all human suffering so near and insistent that the other
aspects of life fade into remoteness" (243). But she is not idealized

nor is she presented as an angel of mercy. Even while Gerty selflessly comforts Lily, she struggles against her jealousy of Lily's beauty and popularity. Although Gerty's concern for others and her independence as a "new woman" are more attractive than Lily's weakness and parasitism, Gerty never upstages Lily. Lily has a magnetism and a sexual vitality that compensate for some shortcomings in character and that gain sympathy for Lily in a way that Gerty's dedication does not.

Simon Rosedale is a more complex character than some critics have judged him to be. According to Walter Rideout and Geoffrey Walton, he is a coarse and evil man designed to contrast with Selden and his fineness of spirit.[2] They, therefore, see Lily's greatest degradation in her eventual willingness to marry Rosedale in order to survive. Actually, anti-Semitism can account for much of Rosedale's social unacceptability. Even in the early part of the book, when Lily perhaps shares such prejudice, she also perceives certain formidable qualities in Rosedale. She recognizes an insecurity and ambition like her own in his attempt to get ahead in the high society. She resents his awareness of her strategies, but she turns first to him rather than to Selden when her financial and social situation becomes desperate. Rosedale resembles Lily, as Elmer Moffat resembles Undine Spragg in *The Custom of the Country* (1913); both Moffat and Rosedale, who begin as totally negative figures, become candid appraisers of social hypocrisy who manage by their shrewdness to control, in part, the society that initially scorns them.

As Lily grows in perception through her suffering, her view of Rosedale alters. She detaches herself from the shallow standards by which he has been condemned, and she appreciates his clumsy concern for her illness, fatigue, and poverty. His urging her to blackmail Mrs. Dorset reveals his ability to fight an unscrupulous society on its own terms. By so doing, he teaches Lily its ruthlessness — something that Selden has never been capable of discerning. Rosedale was stronger than the "trivial society" because he judged it even while he was trying to invade it. The lethargic Selden, who thought he rejected its values, was trapped by it from birth.

Looking back after thirty years at the writing of this novel, Edith Wharton recounted in *A Backward Glance* her struggle to fight off "subordinate themes . . . crowding to the front" and, along with them, characters irrelevant to her purpose (207). She used some of these ideas and figures, however, to suggest the divergent aspects of

New York society. Beyond the aristocrats, the moneyed established society, and the invaders, Edith Wharton depicts the cheap restaurant patronized by secretaries and music students, the dingy boardinghouse, the scrubwoman supporting her invalid husband, the small factories that depend on the exploitation of labor, and the slums with their sickly people. In *The House of Mirth* Mrs. Wharton documents changes in society at large as industrialism and financial speculation accelerated, and she also documents the New York aristocracy's resistance to such change.

When Edith Wharton explores subordinate themes and creates minor characters, she does so only as they relate to Lily and her situation. She uses a unified point of view to the extent that, as Lily moves from the mansions and yachts of millionaires to the rooming houses of the slums, each level of society registers through her eyes. But each social group and Lily's experience with it filter through the eyes of at least one other person. This technique not only adds perspective to Lily's situation but also helps characterize the observer by contrasting his outlook and his behavior with those of Lily. Lily's point of view, though always dominant, is tempered by being held against another's point of view.

Point-of-view characters are not similar to one another in this novel, as James would have insisted they be: They come from different classes and age groups. For Lily as the beautiful and impoverished aristocrat, the parties at Bellmont, the Trenor's estate, are exciting; for Selden as the languid young aristocrat, they are a waste; for Aunt Julia Peniston as the staid and elderly aristocrat, they lead girls toward immorality; for Nettie Struther as the young girl from the slums, they are balls attended by fairy princesses, which she enjoys vicariously in the newspaper accounts of them; and to Simon Rosedale as the vulgar millionaire, they are fortresses to assail. Lily looks condescendingly at Rosedale, but her view of him is not the same as that of others who snub him; and she eventually recognizes in him an opportunism akin to her own. Unlike Gerty Farish, Lily looks at the poor from a distance, even after she herself becomes poor. Selden apparently never sees the poor.

Another aspect of Edith Wharton's mastery of her craft is the creation of minor characters with the greatest precision and economy — a technique she had already perfected in her short stories. Grace Stepney, for instance, registers immediately as a sharply defined individual when Mrs. Wharton observes that she has a mind "like a kind of moral fly-paper, to which the buzzing items of gossip were drawn" (196). Though Mrs. Peniston is always in the background, she is also distinctly presented as Mrs. Wharton defines her personality in terms of the objects that she cherishes. Her furniture symbolizes her solid, old-fashioned stability, and it even persuades us of the reality of her shock when she hears the news of Lily's gambling debts. As she sits alone, convinced that Lily has degraded her, her agitation seems to spread to the objects around her in the darkening parlor. She cannot fight immorality because it is as offensive to admit bad thoughts to her mind as to admit "a smell of cooking in the drawing-room" (204). She is as much a slave to propriety in her moral philosophy as she is in the circumstances of her daily experience.

Similarly, it is through physical objects (this time houses and property) that we see the Wellington Brys so precisely. Their ostentatious habits and their compulsive concern to rise in society are implicit in this one remark that describes their opulent mansion and its scarcely authentic furnishings: "One had to touch the marble columns to learn they were not of cardboard, to seat one's self in one of the damask-and-gold arm-chairs to be sure it was not painted against the wall" (212). Through minor characters, Edith Wharton reflects the amenities and the hollow pursuits of the rich at the same time that she reflects the viciousness of these people toward each other.

Because Edith Wharton develops two main themes — Lily's destruction by her society and her victory over self-centered motives — she emphasizes not only the power that a materialistic culture exerts upon Lily, but also Lily's increasing insight, assurance, and sympathy for others. Though repeatedly a victim of circumstance, Lily must remain a free and unpredictable woman. An ambivalent individual, she acts freely and is also acted upon.

Although Edith Wharton, in the main, clearly develops these principal themes, she sometimes obscures them by attributing Lily's fate to contradictory causes. At times, Mrs. Wharton seems to endorse Lily's own view of her situation when Lily sees herself as the fated heroine of a Greek tragedy. At other times, she sees Lily's conflict in Judaeo-Christian terms in which the individual's own nature can become a battleground for the struggle between good and evil. At still other times, Lily is the protagonist of a Naturalistic novel: forces of cosmic magnitude threaten to overpower her as she becomes the helpless victim of the hypocritical rich.

Edith Wharton, as omniscient author, usually expresses these principal interpretations of Lily's situation, but sometimes, far less appropriately, Lily and Selden voice them. Lily is, after all, a woman who lives for pleasure, who delights in society, and who is hardly a speculative intellectual. It is doubtful, therefore, that she would speak with familiarity about the philosophical implications for her own situation of Greek tragedy. Mrs. Wharton perhaps sensed this incongruity when Lily dramatizes her situation as one pursued by the Furies after Trenor's attempt to rape her. Since she is hysterical to the point of faintness, she would hardly conceive her terror in precise literary terms. In order to make Lily's reference to the classics more credible, Mrs. Wharton parenthetically remarks that Lily had once in a bored moment picked up a copy of Aeschylus that someone had left behind in a guest room. Nevertheless, Lily's impression of the Greek plays, we are to gather, is so powerful that at times of crisis she cries out in horror at the Fates whom she imagines standing in the corners or pursuing her with clanging iron wings.

At other times of stress, Lily becomes acutely conscious of an almost schizophrenic split in her identity: forces of good and evil contend within her. As an Episcopalian, she is a nominal Christian, but she has never connected her own situation with Christian precepts. Part of the drama in the novel arises when she does so, suddenly and intensely; she realizes at a moment of crisis the need to overcome the evil that is part of herself. In fact, when she calls on Selden before her death, she had planned to carry through her project of blackmail and to relinquish her struggle against the evil in her own nature — to commit a kind of moral suicide in order to survive in the physical and social world. But she discovers she cannot so separate the contrasting sides of her nature, and she throws the incriminating letters into the fire. She must live with her split identity as a human being who must perpetually struggle to accommodate the good self and the bad self. Even at the point of death, she drives herself to pay her debts before retiring because she is not sure that her good self will be strong enough to withstand her evil nature in the morning.

Edith Wharton suggests that Lily's inherited tendencies and her early training make her helpless once she is thrust outside a parasitic existence in the houses of the rich. She is unable, as she finds out, to survive economically by her independent efforts as a wage earner. As a fixture of a hedonistic and fashionable society, she has become too specialized to do so, and she finally realizes, with some sense of despair, her limitations in adapting to change. When she is no longer in her niche, she is, as she explains in her farewell visit to Selden, a screw or cog which has fallen out of its machine. Even more strikingly, Edith Wharton uses biological images to suggest Lily's final helplessness before cosmic forces, "an organism as helpless out of its narrow range as the sea-anemone torn from the rock" (486). Lily is often not in command of her destiny; sometimes she is defeated by her emotions, her inclinations, and her personal weakness, sometimes by chance and impersonal social forces. Lily's behavior toward the millionaire Percy Gryce early in the novel provides an example of her drifting in accord with her impulses and shifting moods. Although she senses that he is ready to propose to her, she breaks an engagement with him and goes for a walk with Selden because "the whole current of her mood" carries her toward him. Lily ought perhaps to assume more responsibility for such actions than she does, but Mrs. Wharton prefers to interpret her indiscretion as a determinist might and to see Lily as "a waterplant in the flux of the tides." Ironically, her selfless acts, which are the result of moral choice, contribute to her destruction as much as her irresponsible behavior does. Selden, also a person incapable of acting responsibly and decisively, cannot rise above his excessive caution and his moods of the moment.

Despite the fact that Lily is finally defeated by weakness in the self and by the malignance of an inflexible society, she does actually reveal a remarkable degree of versatility and adaptability. She simply does not possess these qualities sufficiently to survive in a ruthless society which entails for her changes that are too abrupt and too radical for her to cope with. Examples of her versatility abound. Posing in white draperies in the "tableaux vivants" at the Brys party, she delights Gerty and Selden as the Lily they know. But her unadorned figure startles others who cannot connect the image of simplicity which she projects with the sophisticated Lily of their acquaintance. Gus Trenor, hypocritical in his lustfulness, complains that the white gown, which reveals the fluid lines of her figure, is in "damned bad taste," although it appeals to his sensual nature.

Lily seeks to appear under a different guise to each person who knows her, as if she were an actress with multiple roles in her repertoire to entertain a changing audience. She wants Selden to see her as a candidate for his "republic of the spirit." Gerty must see her as one who cares for the poor. Percy Gryce is expected to see her as a scholar who shares his interest in rare books and as a saint who walks demurely to church in a gray dress. Edith Wharton describes Lily as

CARNEGIE LIBRARY
LIVINGSTONE COLLEGE
SALISBURY, N. C. 28144

"perfect" to each of her acquaintances; she is "subservient to Bertha's anxious predominance, goodnaturedly watchful of Dorset's moods, brightly companionable to Silverton and Dacey" (308). Selden, who observes her on a trip to Europe with the nouveau riche, recognizes that a hidden desperation prompts Lily to adapt, chameleon-like, to the moods and impulses of her companions.

As a writer imbued with the ideology of Darwin and the Naturalistic novelists, Mrs. Wharton also interprets Lily's defeat in terms of impersonal social and cosmic forces. The novel illustrates the power of society to destroy even those who, like Lily, possess character and tenacity. As Blake Nevius notes,[3] the cause of each of her downward movements in the social hierarchy is slight; the result is ironically disproportionate because impersonal factors determine so much of the outcome. Lily cannot evade the conventions that govern the exclusive and conservative society to which she belongs at first nor can she evade the economic realities that govern the working class. In her struggles she is defeated, in part, by a universe indifferent to the welfare of any individual or social group.

If Edith Wharton, as she herself recognized, learned much about her craft in writing *The House of Mirth*, she did not altogether master it in this novel. She overworks the element of ironic coincidence so that Lily may begin each stage of her life in a different social class, but she also reveals great skill in the composition of this book. She is expert in using contrasting scenes to balance one another, in coordinating simultaneous actions, in echoing late in the book earlier incidents, and in modulating carefully her dominant themes. In any case, Lily's struggle to survive, to find integrity, and to forgive her enemies lifts *The House of Mirth* beyond topical interest to make it a novel of universal import and lasting appeal.

CHAPTER 3

"A Growing Sense of Mastery"

A FTER *The House of Mirth* appeared, Edith Wharton declared in *A Backward Glance,* her "growing sense of mastery made the work more and more absorbing" (293). Though surrounded now with friends in Paris and Lenox, she recalled "the core of my life was under my own roof, among my books and my intimate friends. Above all, it was in my work, which was growing and spreading." During the next five years, her vision expanded as she experimented with varied subjects and patterns of construction. If *The Fruit of the Tree* (1907) reflects her new interest in the fiction based on social problems and a somewhat Freudian interpretation of marital conflict, *Madame de Treymes* (1907) and *The Reef* (1912) demonstrate her interest in adapting for her own purposes the techniques and the themes used by Henry James.

I The Fruit of the Tree *(1907)*

In *The Fruit of the Tree* Edith Wharton analyzes the psychological complexities of marriage. An awareness of social and moral problems, akin to that undergirding the fiction of her contemporaries like Upton Sinclair and Jack London, also informs the novel. She raises such issues as factory safety, medical care for workers, the unsavory relationship between factories and their insurance companies, the protection of female employees, the caring for children of women workers, and the agonizing dilemma of euthanasia.

Despite her concern with social issues and her penetrating examination of marital conflict, she is unable to encompass these materials in a satisfying form. The structure evinces her recurring interest in the double plot, a technical device she never mastered. Almost all critics agree that she failed to integrate the two strands of the action. The novel at first simplistically contrasts Bessie Westmore, a wealthy widow who owns the textile mill, and Justine Brent, an industrial nurse who has long shared the concern for factory reform felt by John Amherst, an engineer. Fortunately, Bessie develops into more than the clinging, petulant woman, who contrasts with the independent Justine. Once married to Amherst, Bessie fights for what she wants; the spoiled child becomes a demanding, proud, impulsive woman. Paradoxically, she meets defeat in any confrontation because she cannot withstand male disapproval — from her father, her lawyer, or Amherst; she never grows beyond her tendency to weep, scheme, and bargain. She envies the freedom that a divorced friend of hers enjoys, but she is incapable of pursuing a career to gain freedom for herself. In fact, she disdains the woman who works for her livelihood, and she no more admires Justine Brent for pursuing her career as a nurse than Lily Bart admires Gerty Farish for becoming a social worker.

The second half of the book fails to develop organically from the first in plot, character, and theme. At the moment of greatest stress in the marriage of John Amherst and Bessie, Bessie suffers a gratuitous accident and dies. In anger Amherst has left for South America just before Bessie is thrown from the unruly horse he has forbidden her to ride. Abruptly, the interest shifts from the personal conflicts of Amherst and Bessie and from the frustration of his plans for the mill. Justine Brent becomes his second wife, but she does not remain an admirable contrast to Bessie. As a nurse, she must obey male doctors, even when one falsely describes an industrial injury in an insurance record and a second one, Wyant, blackmails her. Dr. Wyant knows that she gave Bessie an excess amount of sedative the night of her death to enable her to escape the intense pain and hopeless paralysis. Justine loses courage and weakly submits to the blackmailer. Later, she shocks Amherst when she confides to him that she administered the fatal medication to Bessie. Although he had deserted Bessie, and although Justine alone had been left to comfort Bessie and make decisions about her care, Amherst is unable to understand Justine's motives; and she is, in turn, shocked by his limited understanding. She sees that he can understand her no better than he did Bessie.

Though Justine has for years been Amherst's companion, confidante, and co-worker, she proves too strong and decisive to be a satisfactory wife for him. He now creates in his mind a Bessie who never was — a suppliant saint, a woman whom he could perfectly love were she to appear again before him. We expect the intelligent, independent Justine of the earlier part of the novel to recognize that Amherst is only seeking to expiate his guilt at deserting Bessie. Instead, Justine becomes a submissive woman who devotes herself to Bessie's child in seeming penance for a guilt that she does not feel. Neither Justine nor Amherst retains credible identity or consistency between the two halves of the book. Amherst dwindles to a character of secondary importance as the point of view shifts from his to that of Justine. Justine, the bright and compassionate "new woman," unconvincingly loses her strength and independence after Amherst condemns her for having administered the fatal medication.

Despite Edith Wharton's failure to maintain consistency in her characters, she succeeds in her use of detail to reinforce her insights into the characters and in her presentation of the conflicts in Amherst's two unsuccessful marriages. Bessie, for instance, finds the milltown oppressive and the mansion which she has inherited cold and provincial. The details that she notices and reacts to reveal her unrest, isolation, and disappointment. The chandelier in the red satin drawing room suggests to her an unfriendliness; lamps would have lent greater warmth and intimacy. She sees the town's lack of sophistication reflected in the decor of the room with its bronze Indians on velvet pedestals and its familiar prints of landscapes. When she inspects the factory, she observes only details personally distasteful to her — grease, dust, belts, and wheels — and fails to see the room and its machinery through the eyes of a worker or the eyes of a reformer.

Amherst, aware of the beautiful and rich widow's limited vision, adjusts his own vision to hers and sees familiar surroundings in a critical light. He fears the impression that his mother's modest house will make on the stranger, and he recoils from "the week's wash flaunting itself indecently" and "the expected whiff of 'boiled dinner'" (69). Ironically, physical details suggest Amherst's alienation from Bessie three years later. The clinging and childlike Bessie so resents Amherst's preoccupation with reform, and he so resents her failure to share his aspirations that they separate. The frills of her boudoir, which had once enchanted him as extensions of her mystery and loveliness, are now distasteful. These symbols of femininity have become the measure of his disillusionment, not of the ecstatic emotion he had once experienced with Bessie.

With similar economy, Mrs. Wharton characterizes her minor figures by mentioning two or three details. Mrs. Truscomb's strength and vulgarity, her wealth and dubious pretentiousness, for instance, are all in one phrase: "a large flushed woman in a soiled wrapper and diamond earrings" (29).

Edith Wharton's treatment of marital disagreement and reconciliation is, in this novel, consistently cynical. Amherst learns this most difficult lesson: "compromise is the law of married life" (292). More often the omiscient author in this novel than in her later work, Mrs. Wharton in the following passage reveals the depths of her cynicism about marriage: "Most marriages are a patchwork of jarring tastes and ill-assorted ambitions — if here and there, for a moment, two colours blend, two textures are the same, so much the better for the pattern" (369). Everyday routines keep married people from truly seeing each other, Mrs. Wharton reiterates. Such blindness can keep a union intact, whereas closer knowledge of the spouse can destroy the fragile relationship. Distractions keep Amherst and Bessie from recognizing their separateness and their growing alienation. It is with surprise that Amherst after three years realizes that he and Bessie are strangers, but it is precisely this lack of intimacy and knowledge that has kept them together.

II Madame de Treymes (1907)

In *Madame de Treymes*, a novella which appeared in the same year as *The Fruit of the Tree*, Edith Wharton achieves a more unified effect. She uses American characters in a European background, elaborates a single psychological conflict, observes detail minutely, suggests dialogue that echoes natural patterns of speech, and employs unspoken soliloquies by her point-of-view character. These techniques suggest the Jamesian influence which grows significantly in her next works, *Ethan Frome* (1911) and *The Reef* (1912). Several themes underlie the action and unify the novella: the materialistic exploitation of the Americans by the French; the contrast between the beautiful upper-class French woman's sexual freedom as exemplified in Madame de Treymes, and the rigid control imposed upon her by patriarchal authority and Roman Catholicism; and the contrast between the freedom which Durham and Fanny Malrive enjoy as American Protestants and the strict discipline imposed upon them by their own sense of responsibility toward each other and toward Fanny's child. Edith Wharton's concentration upon only three characters and her consistent use of Durham's point of view throughout this book add to its remarkable unity.

In a slow beginning, three pages pass while in the elevator Fanny

Malrive buttons the gloves she had carelessly forgotten to put on before leaving her home, an oversight "charged with significance to Durham," who hopes to marry her following her divorce from Madame de Treymes' brother. But Edith Wharton's characteristic concentration and economy surface immediately after Durham's opening reverie. In the Tuileries gardens the conversation of Durham and Fanny focuses on the pivotal forces in the plot; her resolve to keep her only son close to her influence, her indefinable fear that her relationship with the boy may be threatened by her husband's family, and her hesitation to remarry because of this fear.

Because Fanny is apprehensive about the family's probable disapproval of the divorce and her remarriage, Durham elicits its support through an appeal to Madame Christiane de Treymes, Fanny's sister-in-law. She surprises him by agreeing immediately to plead his case, if he pays debts for her lover, who stands on the brink of disgrace. Shocked at her proposal, Durham refuses to associate Fanny's name with an unsavory situation, even to further his own happiness. To his further surprise, Madame de Treymes announces on the next day that she has already persuaded the family to approve the divorce; and her only reward, she now says, will be in watching his happiness when he returns to marry Fanny. Later, Durham learns that Christiane's reward, ironically, will be her vengeful watching of his misery because the family approval of the divorce underlies a conspiracy to gain custody of the child should Fanny ever remarry. Christiane coolly advises Durham against enlightening Fanny about this plan. He can later comfort Fanny, Christiane believes, by fathering a son to replace the one whose custody she will have lost. Christiane seems bewildered that Durham cannot marry Fanny at the price of such deception.

The presence and strength of Christiane de Treymes change the focus of the book from Fanny's conflict to Durham's dilemma. Fanny never needs to decide between Durham and her son because Durham and Madame de Treymes work out her destiny for her, as though she were a symbol in an algebraic equation. Christiane professes love for Fanny and good will toward Durham; yet she is, in reality, self-centered and resentful of the restrictions imposed upon her by the society that will not permit her to divorce an incompatible husband. Both a magnetic and a sinister woman, Christiane is the moving force behind a social conspiracy and may later be its chief victim.

III The Reef *(1912)*

Like classical drama, to which Henry James compared it, *The Reef* develops in five equal sections. Book I is confined to a few days in October, mostly in Givre, Anna Leath's château. The action begins swiftly, as one of Edith Wharton's short stories might. During a spring rain on a Dover pier, the thirty-seven-year-old American diplomat, Darrow, casually meets Sophy Viner, a young girl who has just lost her situation with Mrs. Murrett, a rich American of doubtful reputation. Three months earlier, Darrow had felt his youthful love for the recently widowed Anna Leath revive. He experiences no compunctions, however, in crossing the Channel with Sophy; in attending the theater with her; and, when she discovers the family she was to contact in Paris is out-of-town, in asking the penniless and stranded woman to rest in the room adjoining his hotel suite. He tells himself that Sophy is a child for whom he is providing a holiday, but, in the last paragraph of Book I, when she brings him a letter from Anna late at night, he drowsily kisses her and throws Anna's letter, unread, into the fire.

Tension increases as Darrow arrives some weeks later at Givre, where Anna has been struggling to attain family approval for the betrothal of her stepson, Owen Leath, to the new governess (for Anna's daughter). Madame Chantelle, Anna's mother-in-law, must approve the betrothal because Owen will inherit the family estate upon his marriage. The governess and intended bride, Darrow soon discovers, is none other than Sophy Viner. Though free in his own conduct, Darrow now is surprisingly conventional. Because of their affair in Paris, he does not respect her and he suspects her of marrying Owen for money. He cannot, of course, tell Anna the reasons for his disapproval of Owen's plans. Ironically, Sophy refuses, in Book IV, to discuss plans for her wedding with Owen and mysteriously asks to leave Givre, because she has discovered that she still loves Darrow and wishes to keep her memory of their affair intact.

Sophy is not the only sensitive, imaginative woman in the novel; for Anna Leath also has a Jamesian sixth sense which enables her, like Maggie Verver in *The Golden Bowl*, to divine the previous intimacy of the man she loves with another woman. Accordingly, in Book V, Anna also renounces her wedding plans. Mrs. Wharton then traces Anna's intense inner conflict as she gradually learns to accept Darrow after she can no longer idealize him and as she learns in the process to accept her own passionate, though repressed, nature. Her growth has its limits because her tolerance has limits, and she never accepts Sophy as a human being.

Anna's condemnation of Sophy does not reflect pharisaical sexual or class propriety on Edith Wharton's part so much as her recognition that, in 1912, Anna, like most strictly reared women, still lived in a Victorian world where "people with emotions were not visited." Though presented as a woman of charm and grace, Anna remains a prisoner of inhibitions, narcissim, and rigid mores. Like May Archer in *The Age of Innocence,* Anna is passionate, jealous, and possessive in her love; and, like May, she is both limited and protected by convention.

Through a flashback technique at various points in the novel, Mrs. Wharton economically reveals the origins of Anna's complex nature and of her present reactions to Sophy by showing Anna as she was before her first marriage. Interested even then in Darrow, she had tried to appear unemotional, though she had longed to kiss him; and she mistakenly thought that her lack of demonstrated ardor would awaken his passion. At this point, Darrow had felt attracted to her but not to the extent of being willing to surrender his bachelor freedom; and Anna had become intensely jealous of less inhibited and less proper women who win their men. When Anna Leath learns in Book V of Sophy's affair with Darrow, she experiences a resurgence of her frustrated desire and of her acute jealousy of "freer" women that she had felt some twenty years earlier.

With Darrow's return to Givre, her awareness of sensation becomes abnormally keen as she feels her former passion for him gain ascendancy over her. In her marriage to Fraser Leath, a man of cool temperament, her emotions had found sublimation in affection for her little girl and for her stepson. Darrow notes with some satisfaction that, while Anna indicates no regret that she chose the quiet Leath, who had painted water-colors and collected enamelled snuff boxes, she speaks of him impersonally as if he were some historical figure or a character in a book she had read. However, every detail that connects her with Darrow becomes sexually charged: She finds that his letters give a keener edge to her senses as she touches the paper; she hears not only the sound of his step but the echo of it; she hears his voice from a distance before anyone else does. As he approaches, she feels the plants that she arranges become suffused with vital energy: "Every sensation of touch and sight was thrice-alive in her. The gray-green fur of the geranium leaves caressed her fingers" (106). Even Darrow's coat and hat mingled with hers on a bench suggest to her exacerbated psyche "a sense of homely intimacy."

Wonder pervades her inner being at her present sensuous awakening, even though she is at the same time fearful of some of its implications. She is almost overwhelmed by the "distance" between what she is now and what she had only recently been. She feels some regret as she sees the shadows under her eyes and realizes that her youthfulness is passing. So strong is her love for Darrow, however, and so confident is she in the strength of his passion for her that she dismisses such passing moods of insecurity. No longer guarded in her attitude toward him, she becomes vulnerable to the shock of learning that he had recently taken Sophy as his mistress. She cannot believe that an experience in the past can be relegated to the past; for her, it must, of necessity, have its repercussions in the present. She is torn between a desire to obliterate all thought of Sophy and an obsession to ferret out every detail of the relationship between her and Darrow. Anna is not at all reassured when Darrow makes light of the affair as only a moment's diversion. For Anna, such an admission is only a sign of Darrow's callousness, insensitivity, and masculine complacency.

The psychic interplay between Anna and Darrow and Anna's anguished introspection after she divines the truth in Book V account in large part for the richness of the novel. Darrow at first recognizes that fear keeps Anna from facing reality, but he later reproaches her for not trying to understand his vulnerability to sexual attraction the previous spring. When she cries that she does not *want* to understand, he charges her with a failure in imagination and sympathy. She assumes, in fact, that he regards her as emotionally cold.

At this point, he shifts abruptly and illogically from his halfhearted defense of Sophy's impulsive response to him, from his honest appraisal of his part in their affair, and from his resentful censure of Anna for her lack of understanding of passionate behavior. He begins what even he must recognize as a dishonest placating of Anna, although he, like Anna, is trapped in the conventional pattern of thinking that categorizes women as either "fallen" or "pure." Later, however, he admits to Anna that, while he took it lightly, Sophy saw their affair as no "slight and surface thing." He chides Anna for priding herself on her ignorance of all behavior between men and women that differs from her limited range of experience.

He strives to make her see that living involves compromise. Rather superciliously, Darrow contends that he has already expiated his action by suffering the humiliation of having to explain the old affair to his betrothed.

Anna vacillates in renouncing and in accepting Darrow. Finally, she accompanies him to Paris with the wedding plans again scheduled. In the train compartment, however, her shyness overcomes her urge to express passion and tenderness, and she again becomes the inhibited Anna of her youth. She pretends to read, so that she can maintain a proper dignity and distance and can avoid meeting his eyes; but a second later she resents his reading, as if it presages that he will soon take their love as a matter of course. Her desire for him is so great that she feels misery and dread, even when he leaves her for a moment to buy a newspaper. As he kisses her, leaning in through the window of her cab, she momentarily feels self-reproach at her triumph because she remembers the cry of Sophy Viner who has lost him: "I knew all the while he didn't care."

Had the book ended here, the reader could identify with Anna Leath in her victory as she regains Darrow's love and her love for him and she attains some compassion toward Sophy. But the last two short chapters undercut Anna's largesse, magnanimity, and generosity and reveal her as all too human. Nevertheless, what she loses in spiritual stature she gains in credibility. She broods over the fact that Sophy, through her impulsive and total surrender to Darrow, found emotional experience of an intensity that Anna may never in her reserve be able to emulate. Torn by jealousy, Anna peremptorily demands that Darrow recount every detail of his liaison with Sophy. He recoils from Anna and refuses to satisfy her curiosity and unacknowledged demand for vicarious experience.

Anna is fascinating to analyze as she vacillates in her feelings toward Sophy — from jealousy, to revulsion, to curiosity, to sympathy, to magnanimity, and to dissimulation. Since Anna cannot let her rival alone, the next morning she seeks Sophy at her sister's shabby hotel to tell her that she is relinquishing Darrow to her. This gesture is idle, for the sister announces that Sophy has just left for India with her former employer, Mrs. Murrett. Sophy's sister, a singer, is undoubtedly a courtesan, and she foreshadows for Anna what Sophy may with the years become. The visit thus provides Anna with the rationale to disregard Sophy as an individual and to reject her as one whose destiny will embrace easy living, luxury, and promiscuity.

Henry James enthusiastically praised *The Reef* for its psychological unity and intensity, and he admired its heroine, Anna Leath, as "an exquisite thing . . . a wonder of delicacy." The reverberations of a single situation upon four characters, the psychological interplay between Anna Leath and George Darrow, the long unspoken soliloquies, the economical dialogue, and the delicate adjustment of Anna's idealized views to new emotional experience again reveal the influence of James. Yet the frequent alternating of point of view between Darrow and Anna seems to indicate that Edith Wharton never rigidly followed the precepts of another author.

As in James's work, the turning points in the lives of the characters derive from an individual's sensitive reaction to scenes in which nothing seems to be happening. Owen Leath, for instance, suspects something amiss when, looking up at the library window, he observes Darrow who is having his first meeting alone with Sophy at Givre. Though Owen is beyond the range of hearing, he perceives their agitation because Darrow's head is buried in his hands and because Sophy stands looking fixedly away from him. Anna similarly reveals the same sharpened perception when she tests Owen's suspicion that Darrow and Sophy have previously known each other. After her casual mention of Owen's "foolish" notion to Darrow and Sophy, she expects them to look at each other in surprise. Instead, their studied avoidance of each other's gaze gives her a sure indication that they have been previously acquainted and have hidden this fact.

As in Edith Wharton's earlier novels, background reinforces action and mood. Givre stands for the tradition that supports, as well as inhibits, Anna and for the loveliness, the dignity, and the orderliness that she seeks to maintain in her life and the lives of those around her. It contrasts with Darrow's unattractive hotel suite in Book I, with the lavish surroundings of the newly rich Americans in Europe, like Mrs. Murrett, and with the untidy room inhabited by Sophy's sister. The description of Fraser Leath's small library, where so many crucial conversations occur, emphasizes the stability he had provided for Anna before his death and which she had found reassuring in her life with him. Anna, in fact, needs for her fulfillment *both* the solidity of Fraser Leath and the "winds of passion" brought by Darrow who, perhaps symbolically, plans to take her to South America to live. That her new love builds on the sure but static love of her first marriage is communicated only by suggestion and never by direct statement. Almost no minor characters distract the reader from Anna, Darrow, Sophy, and Owen. Anna's little girl gets no attention; Madame de Chantelle exists only as the matriarchal symbol of aristocratic French propriety — as an extension of the house and grounds at Givre; Adelaide Painter, the forceful American spinster whose advice about other Americans is always consulted, provides humor, but her caricature seems somehow obtrusive. The mood and pace, the evenly sustained tone, and the beauty and orderliness of the château and its grounds reinforce Anna's serenity in the early part of the novel; and they provide an ironic contrast for her growing anxiety in Books Three and Four and for her shock and anguish in Book Five.

Darrow sees Anna as a woman "still afraid of life, of its ruthlessness, its danger and mystery," even after she has been able to acknowledge her passion for him; and her world is, therefore, necessarily limited. Even Mrs. Murrett's shabby gentility and dubious morality seem so remote from Anna that they hardly touch her, and in some ways she seems to be in a different universe from Mrs. McTarvie-Birch, Sophy's disreputable sister. Because of this novel's constricted scene and its intense psychological probings, *The Reef* contrasts with *The House of Mirth, The Custom of the Country*, and, to a lesser degree, with *The Age of Innocence*. In *The Reef* Mrs. Wharton sacrifices much of the dramatic power and the verisimilitude that might have resulted from placing the action in a more representative and more inclusive milieu. She did achieve a compression and a concentration that are impressive, if a bit disembodied; and she also achieved the classical unities of time, place, and action at some cost but also with a remarkable precision and dexterity.

CHAPTER 4

Three Novellas about the Poor

I *"I wanted to draw life as it really was"*

L IKE the novels discussed in the previous chapter, *Ethan Frome* (1911), *Summer* (1916), and *Bunner Sisters* (1916) provide instances of Edith Wharton's experimentation with widely differing characters, settings, and structural patterns. *Bunner Sisters*, though published (in *Xingu*), concurrently with *Summer*, was written twenty-five years earlier; and it belongs stylistically with her earliest fiction. In all three novellas, Mrs. Wharton focuses upon the lives of the poor in the late 1880's; and she poignantly demonstrates how they must settle for survival and frustration when they can attain nothing else.

A character in each novella takes responsibility for someone else, even at the expense of his own well-being and regardless of whether or not the person he helps is deserving or lovable. The central figures in these books do not achieve mastery; they learn to endure. The fact that people in constricted situations may be selfless is the only solace that Mrs. Wharton offers, but some people, such as Charity Royall in *Summer*, do not progress so far. If anything, characters motivated by unselfishness and responsibility suffer more than the selfish and irresponsible. In Mrs. Wharton's view, life begins unhappily for the deprived, they move through "crucial moments" of intense suffering, and they simply continue to live after the drama of life for them has dissipated. Neither villains nor heroes emerge in these novellas. While comic touches abound, they are sardonic and deepen the mood rather than lightening it.

Though *Bunner Sisters* takes place in New York, Edith Wharton sought in *Ethan Frome* and *Summer*, as she declared in *A Backward Glance*, "to draw life as it really was" in rural Massachusetts and to correct romantic impressions left by the "rose-and-lavender pages of

Mary E. Wilkins Freeman and Sarah Orne Jewett" (293 - 4). In 1922, Mrs. Wharton explained that such New England writers had used the colorful flora and the homespun dialect of their region but had ignored the granite protruding through the grass. Accordingly, she emphasized in *Ethan Frome* the rigor of life in a harsh land with its rocky soil, its cold winters, and its bleak, desolate beauty.[1] In *Summer* she analyzed the stifling effects of New England even upon Charity Royall who loves its landscape.

Since Edith Wharton painstakingly strove for truth of impression in these New England tales, she took issue with critics who assumed that she could write authentically only about aristocratic New York. In *A Backward Glance* she recalls that in 1911 she read *Ethan Frome* to Walter Berry as she wrote it and that together they scrutinized the milieu of the tale for accuracy (296). She established her authority to write about the rural scene on the basis of her ten-year residence at Lenox, her daily excursions into the countryside, and her conversations with a clergyman who ministered to the Bear Mountain community a few miles from her home (this settlement served as prototype for Charity Royall's birthplace).

More to the point is her consistently demonstrated ability to depict people whose daily routines and circumstances are different from her own and to recreate the life of earlier generations, whether in Italy, New York, or Western Massachusetts. Whether she accurately judged how much Ethan would have charged to drive Lockwood (the narrator), how much he would have known about alimony and bank loans, and how the community dances in the village were staged, all matter less than her insight into the psychological effects of rural isolation, her knowledge, as an avid gardener, of the patience demanded of those who work with unproductive soil, and her empathy, as one at that moment preparing for divorce, with Ethan's compulsion to escape a deadening marriage. She knew from living with a sick and difficult spouse that pettiness and anger, more often than nobility, are the results of suffering. The contrast between the beauty of the landscape around Lenox and the "mental starvation" of people who inhabited it disturbed her.[2]

While Edith Wharton observed carefully the people living near her and their surroundings, she recognized that the telephone and automobile had made their lives fuller than those of their parents. Thus both *Ethan Frome* and *Summer,* by design, reflect the deprivations of the preceding generation.

II   *The Harsh Artistry of* Ethan Frome:
"*Without an added ornament*"

In *Ethan Frome* Edith Wharton emphasizes the differences between the present and the recent past by using the young narrator,
Lockwood, who must look back twenty-five years. Distressed by the
duration into late spring of snow drifts and intense cold, he imagines
himself in the place of these people in the recent past when hardship
was even more acute and isolation more complete. While Ethan is
twenty-eight during the main part of the story in Lockwood's
retrospective narrative, he is already fifty-two and prematurely aged
by toil and by the bitter climate when Lockwood first sees him.

Isolated from the world, Ethan Frome's wife, Zeena, naturally
chooses to be sick because sickness promises adventure in its possible
complications, sudden cures, and relapses. The patent medicines she
receives in the mail provide her only excitement and her only relief
from a paralyzing spiritual monotony. She resents Mattie Silver's
vitality and her tendency to daydream more than she fears Ethan's
interest in her. Zeena is tired and needs household help, but Mattie,
the hired girl, lacks efficiency. Zeena is not seen simply as part of
Ethan's curse, as some critics have implied, but as a deprived woman
who grieves over lost beauty when the cherished red pickle dish she
has saved since her wedding is used by Mattie and broken.

The book is fraught with such ironies: the dish that is treasured is
the one that is broken; the pleasure of the one solitary meal that
Ethan and Mattie share ends in distress; the ecstasy of the coasting
ends in suffering; the moment of dramatic renunciation when Ethan
and Mattie choose suicide rather than elopement ends not in
glorious death but in years of pain. The lovely Mattie Silver becomes
an ugly, querulous woman cared for by Zeena, who, again ironically,
finds strength and companionship by caring for her former rival.

Edith Wharton's strenuous attempt to counteract the "rose-and-
lavender" impression of New England which she found in works by
Mary E. Wilkins Freeman and Sarah Orne Jewett, and her refusal to
present her people triumphant over their incessant struggles
alienated critics like John Crowe Ransom, Bernard DeVoto, and
Lionel Trilling who recoiled in particular from *Ethan Frome* and
who contended that Mrs. Wharton excited a reader's sadistic sensibilities.[3] They are so uncomfortable with her objectivity that they
gain little esthetic and spiritual satisfaction from the book. Instead,
they imply that *Ethan Frome* is distinctive for the technical skill that

Mrs. Wharton evinced in it rather than for its vision of human experience. But, if a critic is to value these novellas as literature, he cannot admire their technical dexterity to the exclusion of their truth to the human experience which Mrs. Wharton dramatized in them. During her lifetime, the popularity of *Ethan Frome,* certainly the best-known of her books, caused her some dissatisfaction. She opposed those who insisted that it was her best work and who neglected her more substantial works. Nevertheless, she regarded the book as the fruition of her long search for technical mastery and artistic maturity and contended that she had modulated carefully her structure to the requirements of her materials. The characterization is subtle, strong, and masterful. Her three chief figures have achieved, in the years since it was written, a mythic dimension and seem to be extensions of the grim landscape itself. The ardent lover turned cynic, the beautiful woman turned a soured cripple, and the protective mother figure emerging as a sinister dictatorial presence are all illuminating and arresting conceptions. The very texture of the prose elicits admiration, particularly in the accomplished use of imagery to sustain a moral judgment or to comment implicitly on a character or situation. The blighted apple trees, the rocks sticking out of the soil, the neglected cemetery, the broken cut-glass pickle dish that was a wedding present too good to use, the false teeth that Ethan hates to see beside Zeena's bed, the misshapen remodelled farmhouse that reminds Lockwood of Ethan's crippled back — all are vivid and compelling metaphors in this tale of spiritual deprivations. Yet these deprivations, endured stoically, form the vision of life that Lockwood creates. We cannot, then, separate the technical felicities of the novel — its compelling characterization and its vital imagery — from the experience that Mrs. Wharton sought to enlarge in the work.

Since life was stark rather than rich for her characters, Edith Wharton felt that she must avoid the leisurely elaboration inherent in the novel form and utilize instead the bluntness possible in short fiction. Writing an introduction to a new edition of *Ethan Frome* in 1922, she realized that this conviction conflicted with her usual view that the novel provided the most appropriate genre for any narrative spreading over two generations. In the case of this narrative, she had instinctively realized that the shorter form could alone express the unadorned strength of Ethan Frome and that exhaustive analysis would tend to nullify the stark effect for which she was striving. To encompass Ethan's situation persuasively, she saw that she must present it "without an added ornament, or a trick of drapery or lighting."[4]

In the earliest version of *Ethan Frome*, written in French, she used no character as narrator. In the final version, Lockwood, as narrator, provides a frame to the story and a complicated time scheme by means of which she could dramatically envision the contrast between the bleak existence of her characters in the present with their youthful expectations in the past. Lockwood, more sophisticated than the people he observes, learns gradually about the tragedy from several simple, relatively inarticulate persons; for each of the villagers tells him as much about the situation as he can understand. His more sophisticated intelligence, then, synthesizes these complicated and mysterious fragments into a single *vision* which gives order to the myriads of facts and impressions that others have presented to him. Possessing "scope enough to see it all," he is, in effect, a kind of artist in his own right. Lockwood's own character is important in helping him fulfill his task. He is never the factual reporter; he is the curious, meditative, expansive sensibility who feels ready sympathy for the wasted Ethan Frome when he first observes him and who associates the bleakness in Ethan's face with his own reaction to the harsh winter. In Lockwood's endeavors to withstand the benumbing influence of coldness and isolation upon his own spirit, he finds strength in actively sympathizing with Ethan, Zeena, and Mattie. His human warmth, perhaps, prevents his own spiritual relapse.

As an engineer who constantly daydreams, Lockwood can identify with Ethan who had attended a technical school and who had found the beginnings of a sustaining illusion in his work in the laboratories. But, as an outsider and a member of another generation, Lockwood is remote enough from Ethan's tragedy to see it in perspective, much as it appalls him. Lockwood's seeing Ethan's youthful promise at a distance deepens the implications of his tragedy because time only dulls Ethan's wounds but does not cure them. He has had to learn to endure, and time has only accentuated his suffering instead of alleviating it. Because the tragedy continues to ramify from the past into the present through the sensibilities of an imaginative narrator, mundane survival for Ethan and Mattie becomes more horrible in its impact than their sudden death would have been. As a result of their suicide pact, Mattie and Ethan exchange a hoped for life-in-death for a demeaning death-in-life when their attempt fails. How overwhelming their defeat has been, Mrs. Wharton fully actualizes by presenting it obliquely through the eyes of a young stranger.

III Summer: *"Confusedly . . .
what might be the sweetness of dependence"*

In *Summer*, as in *Ethan Frome*, the principal character, Charity Royall, aspires to escape from a stultifying community. She has a brief love affair, faces pregnancy alone, and eventually resigns herself to a life of emotional barrenness as the bride of her elderly guardian. Unlike Ethan, Charity lacks any sense of responsibility or affection for those with whom she lives, and she remains in North Dormer because she cannot otherwise survive. She never contends against nature as a hostile force, as Ethan does, but identifies with it as a source of moral and spiritual strength, rather than with people. Nature reinforces her assurance early in the book and sustains her in her later desperation. She responds to it with ecstasy, savoring the roughness of the dry mountain grass on her skin, the smell of thyme crushed against her face, and the songs of birds. She lies in the grass "immersed in an inarticulate well-being," reaches out to the light of the morning sun when she wakes, and feels her turbulent spirit at one with the storms. Within herself, she knows that she is part of a larger universe through this affinity with the physical world surrounding her.

Others in North Dormer, a village two blocks long, do not share this sort of mystical exaltation. Not only are the land and climate characterized by rigor but so are the standards that regulate the social existence of its people. Class lines are even more inhibiting for them when they wish to marry than such barriers would be in high urban society. The double standard for sexual behavior is sometimes devastating in this claustrophobic village. There, people cannot escape the circumstances of their birth and heredity or the traditions that enclose them. The mountain which looms threateningly over those who, like Charity, leave its alienated group of outcasts to live in North Dormer is symbolic of the inhibiting forces of rural tradition and inflexible ancestral ways. Those who suffer most from alienation often intensify their own isolation; such is the paradox informing the lives of the mountain people who refuse to admit strangers from the village below to their homes and who inspire distrust in all who approach.

Like Ethan, Lawyer Royall, Charity's guardian, has intellectual curiosity and a thirst for knowledge — attributes that she does not share and tends to scorn. Royall's past emerges through the villagers' shadowy allusions to his drinking, to his interest in women, and to his premature retirement from a city practice. But this intelligent widower, whose wistful interest in a young woman somewhat resembles Ethan's in Mattie, arouses Charity's hostility as she grows up. Not an intellectual, she identifies books only by their covers, considers the public library where she works a prison, and finds bewildering the historical interests of her lover, Harney, an architect who spends a summer in the village. Royall is the most powerful man in town, but he is powerless whenever he faces Charity's rebellion or determination. At the same time that she feels hatred and sexual revulsion for him, she enjoys dominating him. She asserts her cool authority in other ways; for example, when she enters the public library to begin her work, she insolently plants her hat on the bust of Minerva.

But Charity is vulnerable to sexual passion, and her assurance diminishes the first afternoon she meets Harney: "Confusedly, the young man . . . had made her feel for the first time what might be the sweetness of dependence." She allows herself to drift with the force of passion, and eventually she must endure the humiliation of Harney's deserting her and of learning that he is to marry a woman of his own class. Pregnant, Charity seeks help wherever she can hope to find it, first from an abortionist, whose assistant confiscates her money, and then from the inhabitants of the mountain village where she hopes to find her mother, a prostitute whose face she cannot recall. Symbolically, her mother deserts her instead of helping her; she dies in the most sordid surroundings just before Charity arrives. The body lies discolored and bloated on an unmade cot, and boisterous drunks blaspheme nearby. Charity meets Royall on her long walk back to town; and, now that she feels cornered by fate, she agrees to marry him. She faintly acknowledges that he is being kind.

The surface plot follows that of popular sentimental fiction, but its significance strikes deeper. Mrs. Wharton presents the cliché situation of an independent adolescent brought to maturity by a tempestuous love affair, humbled by her lover's desertion, and saved from an abortion and social ostracism by a stable citizen whom she has previously scorned. But Charity's development represents no improvement, for she is no more sensitive to other people than ever, and she still prefers nature to humanity. Her confidence and freedom from inhibition in the past arose from the detachment with which she viewed all others. When she loses this objectivity, she only becomes confused about their human attributes and her own. Even her decision not to get an abortion is a last-moment reassertion of her independence: she rebels against the pressures of a judgmental society. She insists upon keeping what is hers, just as the bird's nest and the warm grass have been hers. She is motivated by an animistic sense that the fetus growing within her links her with the forces of nature — a universe bigger than North Dormer; and, at the very least, the developing baby gives her importance in her own eyes. She is in reality a child of nature, and she regards her unborn child with the protectiveness of a wild animal. But living in a human society, her decision to keep her baby forces her into marriage with a man she has despised, though he is her moral superior in compassion. The age of her guardian, his drinking, and the overtones of incest ominously darken the ending.

Charity's love affair has thus cost her her independence as a human being. She has, in effect, spent her life in one summer. Her passion — beautiful, wild, and brief — exists in memory only as the Fourth of July celebration to which Harney took her continues to exist. That celebration of independence ended in her driving back with Harney to an unchanged, quiet village where the independence she sought was impossible. Similarly, after their marriage, Charity and Royall drive back in cold autumn moonlight. Her summer experience made her aware of the potentiality that emotion holds for a mature woman. In exchange, she lost an inner self-reliance which would have insured her human survival and possibly her escape from both North Dormer and the implacable cosmic forces symbolized by the mountain — forces with which she is in large measure attuned but which also represent a fatality far stronger than she as a limited individual can cope with.

IV Bunner Sisters: *"the inutility of sacrifice"*

Underlying the *Bunner Sisters* are two themes: (1) the sinister nature of poverty and (2) the ironically tragic consequence of unselfish behavior. In illustration of these themes, Ann Eliza Bunner gives her own suitor and her small savings to her sister, Evelina. Since no act of love is totally selfless, Ann Eliza assumes that, as her reward, she will share vicariously in her sister's happiness. Instead, Evelina becomes more remote in her new, presumed affluence; she moves away, and she is condescending and impersonal in her occasional letters.

Mrs. Wharton's sense of the unusual implications of her materials

intensifies continually as the tale moves to its tragic denouement.
Instead of happiness, Evelina experiences misery in her marriage,
and her health fails under the strain. After the broken Evelina
returns home, the thought crosses Ann Eliza's mind that she may
now possess completely her sister's affection and companionship.
But even this modicum of happiness is denied her when she learns
that Evelina is a convert to Roman Catholicism and will, Ann Eliza
assumes, now be separated from her for eternity.

More isolated than ever before, Ann Eliza feels herself a victim of
the irrational forces that control the universe and of the unpredictable aspects of human life and human emotions. She had previously
thought the universe was controlled by predictable moral principles,
one of which was the value of self-sacrifice. The identification of
herself as the cause of the tragedy and of the ever-widening separation between herself and Evelina deepens her sense of alienation and
desolation. Ann Eliza's final realization that all her previous beliefs
had been mistaken is convincing esthetically because Edith Wharton
meticulously emphasizes Ann Eliza's naïveté in her every word, act,
and thought; and her naïveté is intensified by a certain recklessness
and lack of critical sense.

This novella is only a partial success; its stilted dialogue and the
obtrusive presence of the author mark it as early work. But Edith
Wharton's growing artistry is manifest in the exactitude of the
details which she uses to depict the uneventful lives of women who
barely survive as shopkeepers, dressmakers, or milliners. She does
achieve notable effects — a consistency of tone, for example, which
reinforces her conviction that, for the deprived of this world, the
ramifications of one unintended or unwise conversation can lead ultimately to a catastrophe out of all proportion to its inciting cause.
For the poor, there exists no margin of error.

CHAPTER 5

"Particular fine Asperity":
The Custom of the Country

I   The Reckless Picaro

*T*HE *Custom of the Country* is one of Mrs. Wharton's indisputable masterpieces, and she herself always considered the novel among her greatest achievements. She reveals in it an imposing breadth and scope as she ranges over the American and European social scenes, she has created memorable and incisive characters, she evinces much in the way of critical control over her disparate scenes and personages, she manifests a sense of irony which allows her to see her characters in a critical and not altogether unsympathetic light, and she dramatizes impressively the clashes between individuals and cultures by her objectivity. *The Custom of the Country* is undoubtedly the most massive of her books, and it would be her greatest if she had conceived her characters with as much compassion as sardonic irony.

Upon its publication, many critics greeted *The Custom of the Country* as the important book that it is. Henry James praised it highly, as he had *Ethan Frome* and *The Reef* which had immediately preceded it. He liked her hard intellectual touch and her "particular fine asperity." Her prose, he thought, was "almost scientifically satiric."[1] This novel, along with *The House of Mirth* and *Ethan Frome*, assured Mrs. Wharton's lasting fame as a novelist and solidified her reputation among readers and critics alike.

Interesting parallels and contrasts emerge as we compare two of her best books to this date. While Mrs. Wharton had written *The House of Mirth* in six months, she needed more than four years to write *The Custom of the Country*. In both novels she analyzed turn-of-the-century polite life, but, because *The Custom of the Country* covers a decade, she was also able to extend her coverage to include a time a few years later when society had become more fluid. Now the newly rich exert greater power, the aristocrats have grown weaker, and divorce, regarded as disgraceful in the early chapters, is soon commonly to be condoned. Whereas Mrs. Wharton's compassionate treatment of Lily Bart tempered her satire in the earlier book, her detached presentation of Undine, an egocentric woman who flamboyantly pursues her shifting ambitions, imposes a distance between the reader and Undine which precludes sympathetic identification with her.

In contrast to Lily Bart's destruction by a shallow society, Undine's imperturbable victory over it establishes the principal theme. She moves through a series of adventures with, as Nevius suggests, the daring and recklessness of a picaro.[2] She never suffers defeat, only the frustrating discovery that whatever she gains is less satisfying to her after she has it in her grasp. She marries Ralph Marvell because he is a descendant of the exclusive Dagonets, who are "sweller than anybody." But, for one with her predilections, the subtleties of the aristocratic code and its humane if constricted values mean little when she discovers that Peter Van Degen and his fellow Invaders (the newly rich) are "sweller" than the Dagonets. When she discovers that they have yachts and more money, she is insatiable in cultivating them. But things do not always go her way, for, after she divorces Marvell to marry Van Degen, he throws her over. Consequently, she more deliberately engineers her entrapment of Raymond de Chelles, a French nobleman.

But in a sense she overreaches herself in this relationship also; to her chagrin, she discovers after marriage that the European aristocracy inhibits her more than did the New York aristocracy. Frenchmen of noble family, in the custom of a different but withal materialistic country, control their women rigorously, regarding their wives as bearers of sons and as decorative chattels to enhance their own social standing. In Raymond's ancient château in Burgundy, Undine must conform to the stultifying habits of his female relatives who sit dutifully in the courtyard or in the cold halls and work for hours on their exquisite needlework in apathetic silence and who yield all respect to the old marquise and all humility to the men in the family. Because of such a placid life, no channel seemingly exists into which Undine can direct her own boundless, vital energy.

Undine is nothing if not self-willed, strong in the pursuit of power and relentless in her driving ambition. Since the de Chelles family interferes with her prerogatives as she sees them, she has no scruples in abandoning her second husband. She eventually divorces de Chelles to remarry Elmer Moffatt, now a millionaire. The reader gradually learns that Undine and Moffatt had eloped in Apex, but her parents had had the marriage annulled because they thought that he was not good enough for her. If Undine had sought her opposite in Ralph Marvell and Raymond de Chelles, she finds her own kind in Moffatt who also sees in her a kindred spirit, though he is less deceitful. She is still insatiable for high status; and, even after this marriage, she thinks momentarily of divorcing Moffatt to become the wife of an ambassador, until she discovers that divorcées are ineligible for such glory. Undine always wins over the circumstances of the moment, but winning, ironically, is never enough.

In Book I, Edith Wharton introduces the Spraggs and reviews their past lives in Apex, their fear of Moffatt, and their two years of frustrating life in New York. In Book I, which closes with Undine's impending marriage to Ralph Marvell, most of the minor New York and Midwest characters appear and require little elaboration as they weave in and out of the later action. Book II spans the four years between Undine's disappointment with the European honeymoon and her decision to choose Peter Van Degen instead of Raymond de Chelles as a successor to Ralph; but she loves none of the three. Inconveniently for her ambitions and selfish designs, Ralph becomes critically ill; the family summons her, but she goes ahead with her plans (at the end of Book I) to travel to Italy with Van Degen. Van Degen's later discovery that she did not rush to her husband when he needed her makes him decide against marrying her.

Two and a half years elapse between chapters 13 and 14 of Book II, between Undine's discovery of her pregnancy and the day she misses the celebration of Paul's second birthday. Books III and IV extend over the two years between her divorce from Ralph and her marriage to Raymond de Chelles. In Book III, she adjusts to Van Degen's failure to claim her in Reno and launches her successful campaign to become the Marchioness de Chelles. In the shorter Book IV, Edith Wharton focuses solely on Ralph's vain efforts to raise money in order to retain custody of Paul by bribing the avaricious Undine who needs the money to attain an annulment from the Vatican so that she may marry de Chelles. Book IV ends with Marvell's pathetic suicide, a symbolic event denoting the weakness of his class despite the fine moral qualities that Mrs. Wharton has established for him. In Book V, Undine grows disillusioned with her marriage to Raymond de Chelles, and she has no scruples about divorcing him and returning to her "soul-mate," Elmer Moffatt, who can at least offer her excitement, security, and power.

II   *Undine as "the monstrously perfect result of the system"*

"The custom of the country" denotes the prevalent worship of wealth and the power it signifies, a power that can reduce human beings to things and that measures them solely in material terms. American mores encouraged men to value women as possessions and to provide them with the resources for prestige and pleasure in return for their complaisance, companionship, and sexual intimacy. This custom led to Lily Bart's helplessness in adversity; Undine Spragg, on the other hand, exploits these materialistic values to her advantage in her relationships with her father, her lover, and her three husbands. She succeeds in furthering most of her selfish designs in a world that extols virtue and purity but actually rewards beauty and shrewdness. Lily gradually becomes a complex human being; Undine, though more than a caricature, remains less than fully rounded. She is a powerful symbol of physical attractiveness and money used in the service of an insatiable ambition, and she seems less to fight against the inflexible moral standards and conventions than to be unaware of them. Taking for granted that, as a beautiful woman, she can imperiously direct others and thereby achieve her purposes, she sincerely desires the well-being of all those about her, provided they fall in with her own expressed or implied wishes: "If only everyone would be as she wished, she would never be unreasonable" (266).

Undine does not develop as a result of her widening experience; she becomes, in fact, more compulsive in her self-centered activities. She views each adventure separately and not philosophically. Edith Wharton's own satiric vision, however, broadens with Undine's successive experiences because they illuminate the weaknesses of each of the groups with whom she identifies during the course of the novel: the New York aristocracy, the established first-generation rich, the provincial French nobility, and the nouveau riche recently arrived from the Midwest.

Scene is diversified in order to extend the reaches of the novel. In New York it shifts from fashionable Fifth Avenue to the unfashionable Stentorian Hotel to the Wall Street offices of Spragg or Moffatt. Beyond New York, the characters move from Apex to

Opake, Nebraska; to Skog Harbor, Maine; to Reno. Undine spends her honeymoon in Italy, Switzerland, and Paris. Between marriages, she makes two journeys from France to New York. Married to de Chelles, she divides her time between the Burgundian château and the ancient family house in Paris. Her enjoyment of the Nouveau Luxe, where rich and vulgar Americans gather, contrasts with the enforced frugalities practiced at the Hôtel de Chelles. In addition to the shifting milieu, a plethora of minor characters of several nationalities and classes, most of them possessing individualized characteristics, give *The Custom of the Country* its amplitude. These characters add depth and perspective to Undine's activities and offer some continuity to her migrations. The book covers a decade, and successive references to the age of Undine's son establish the passage of time.

Such fullness in *The Custom of the Country* markedly contrasts with the studied unity and focus attained in *The Reef*. In that novel almost no minor figures are present, and the action, after the prelude, is limited to a few days at Givre. Yet Edith Wharton manages, surprisingly, to control the burgeoning energy and size of *The Custom of the Country* with a structure not unlike the one she employed in writing *The Reef*: she again divides her novel into five books and imparts again a sense of the movement characteristic of a five-act drama. Within each of the five sections, individual scenes relate clearly to one another and to an emerging pattern within that section. A single geographical setting and one set of related problems dominate each book and distinguish it from the others. Minor characters establish connections among the books, and so do the flashbacks into a past more remote than the earliest events in the novel, flashbacks which may occur in any of the five books. For instance, Undine never returns to Apex, but Mrs. Wharton sketches her life in Apex and Elmer Moffatt's background there through the recollections, which appear at various points in the novel, of Mr. and Mrs. Spragg, Undine, and Elmer. Frequent references to the Spraggs' fashionably rustic summers in Skog Harbor and Lake Potash extend the canvas of the novel and introduce, with considerable economy, Undine's confidante and advisor, Madame de Trezak.

In addition to this retrospective technique, Edith Wharton makes significant use of another technique of the dramatist — the choric figure who adumbrates, reflects upon, or interprets important events. Mme. de Trezak is such a figure, but more important are

Mrs. Heeny and Charles Bowen. Mrs. Heeny, a *masseuse* for society
people, predicts Undine's future in the opening scene with her advice, "Go steady, Undine, and you'll get anywheres." Apparently
classless, Mrs. Heeny claims to know "everybody" and looks impar-
tially, but sympathetically, upon people in all classes. She cheers up
Mrs. Spragg, explains to Undine the intricacies of invitations and of
replies to them, carries in her bag clippings from the society columns
which keep Undine informed about the activities of her peers and
rivals, and provides Undine with cautionary advice about or encouragement in her enterprises.

Charles Bowen, an anthropologist, observes life with the detachment of a scientist and only occasionally generalizes about his reactions. At one point, for example, he concludes that most men become
slaves in the marketplace in order to give money and social power to
their wives; but the men feel too superior to the women to discuss
their work with them. Ralph Marvell, he stresses, is an exception to
the system; he prefers a leisured, genteel existence and a sharing of
his inner life with his wife. Ralph is not likely, in Bowen's view, to
survive in a shifting cultural scene in which qualities more vigorous
than Marvell's will be at a premium. On the other hand, he regards
Undine as "the monstrously perfect result of the system" which has
tended to discount, in the worship of Mammon and the pursuit of
power, the qualities of integrity and of consideration for others that
Ralph symbolizes. It is Bowen who brings together two cultures,
each motivated by a different kind of materialism, when he introduces Raymond de Chelles to Undine. In so doing, he is
something like the scientist who confines two incompatible kinds of
animals in a cage in order to watch their adaptations to their en-
vironment and to each other.

Some critics have regarded Undine's unscrupulousness as evidence that Midwesterners had brought with them to New York
the excessive materialism, the disregard for morality, and the
deterioration of culture that Edith Wharton thought dominated
modern life. Such a critical view inadequately apprehends her satiric
range; for, she felt, to some extent, that the hypocritical Dagonets of
this world were more vulnerable to close scrutiny than were the more
open and forthright, though admittedly Philistine, Midwesterners.
Similarly, Undine's frank acknowledgment of her financial needs
and her direct approach to economic facts contrast favorably with
Raymond de Chelles' pretenses, his unwillingness to recognize his

poverty, and his resentment of the rich Americans with whom he associates.

Clare Van Degen's refusal to divorce her unfaithful husband and to acknowledge openly her love for Ralph Marvell springs from moral cowardice, from her conviction that divorce is "a vulgar and unnecessary way of taking the public into one's confidence" (322). Mr. Spragg honestly states the principle that almost all the other characters live by: "I guess it's up to both parties to take care of their own skins" (261). But only he recognizes that Undine must return the pearls she accepted from Van Degen. Plump and ridiculous, Mrs. Spragg appeals to one's sympathies because of her "stores of lymphatic patience." Princess Estradina's promiscuity shocks even Undine, despite her awe of royalty. The inescapable fact remains that Edith Wharton satirizes dehumanizing materialism and rampant egotism in whatever social classes in America or abroad these attributes are dominant.

III   *Undine's Vanity: the Need for "a reflecting surface"*

Though self-assured, Undine is, paradoxically, dependent upon others to help her decide what she wants. She identifies closely with the values of whatever group claims her attention, and she assimilates these values in her compulsive desire to dominate the group. In so doing, she illuminates the weaknesses of each group as she mirrors them. Her personality is a kind of "tabula rasa" as she absorbs each time into her own being the prevailing attitudes of those whom she confronts, while she eliminates from her mind the ideas and predilections that had been there previously. She also studies the responses of other people to her actions, waiting for their remarks or changes in facial expression. In this sense, they serve as a mirror to her. There are narcissistic elements in her personality which obtrude when she regards herself in a mirror and rehearses her behavior.

It is no accident that the central image in the book is the mirror. As a child, Undine did not jump rope or play ball; instead, she played lady in front of a mirror. As she prepares for her first New York party, she enacts a pantomime before a mirror. Ralph Marvell's disillusionment on their honeymoon begins with his recognition that she does not want to be alone with him because she needs admiring crowds to provide a "reflecting surface" for her charm. Mr. Popple, the artist who paints society women, through his idealized, impressionistic portrait of her offers her another flattering mirror of herself. When Undine changes her life style by changing her friends and husbands, she does so in order to find more significant mirrors for her beauty and untried ranges of behavior to copy. When she hears that aristocrats consider art to be important, she immediately visits a gallery. She follows a woman in furs, adapting her own facial expression and gestures to hers as she examines each work and makes notes in her guidebook. Only as Undine observes the reactions of others to each of her dramatic actions does she decide whether she has been really victorious or whether she should seek a different prize: "To know others were indifferent to what she had thought important was to cheapen all present pleasure and turn the whole force of her desires in a new direction" (286).

The Custom of the Country encompasses the tragedy of Ralph Marvell's suicide and communicates the poignant loneliness of Undine's son. Nevertheless, the novel remains a comedy of manners that has the tone of a satiric fable. Geoffrey Walton compares the stylized comedy of this novel, with its vigorous caricatures and brilliantly visualized episodes, to Jonsonian drama.[3] As in Ben Jonson's drama, unusual names typify the sardonic surface of Mrs. Wharton's satire. Undine was named for the successful hair tonic that transformed her father from an Apex druggist to a millionaire. Edith Wharton makes one reference to the wavelike suggestion in the name in describing Undine's graceful figure and fluid movements, but she does not connect her with the myth of the undines (water sprites who gain a soul if they marry a mortal and bear a child) except by implication — Undine is incapable of gaining a soul and feels no love for her child. Undine's friends bear caricature-like names: Mabel Lipscomb, Indiana Frusk, Maynard Binch, Lootie Arlington, Roviano, Madame Adelschein, Nettie Wincher, Ora Prance Chettle, Miss Stager, Claud Walsingham Popple, and Bertha Shallum. They come from satirically envisioned places like Phalanx, Georgia; Opake, Nebraska; or Deposit, Kansas.

But Mrs. Wharton's satire extends toward aristocrats as well as Invaders. She treats Marvell's suffering sympathetically when Undine claims Paul, but she is critical of his earlier embarrassment about the sensational press reports of the divorce. She implies that pride causes his irritation at such invasion of his privacy as an aristocrat for the pleasure of the common reader. He simply does not have the strength to ignore scandal or to take it in his stride even though he is

innocent of the charges levelled against him. Particularly annoying
to him is the repeated report that the divorce arose because of his
single-minded devotion to business, since he has been unusually
attentive to his wife and has entered aggressively into real-estate
promotion solely because of her insatiable demand for money. As a
man lacking some ultimate degree of self-sufficiency, he is in the end
more concerned with his reputation in the larger world than with
proclaiming the truth about his situation. Mrs. Wharton also exposes
the failings of the French nobility, notably the men's arrogance
toward women and the women's willingness to efface their individuality at the family's behest. Though Raymond de Chelles
would not acknowledge the truth of the judgment, his behavior
more often suggests inflexibility and hauteur than incorruptibility or
regard for a living culture.

In praising the consistency of tone in this satirical comedy, we
must except the presentation of Ralph Marvell. Mrs. Wharton has
presented his suicide and its attendant circumstances with such intensity that the sequences involving him depart from her characteristic impersonal mode in writing this novel. On the other hand,
she establishes in convincing detail his frustrated aspirations, his disillusionment with Undine, and his possessiveness in regard to Paul
— aspects of the book that communicate the inevitability of his
despair. Through Ralph's eyes, as he gradually learns to see his wife
as she is, Undine develops into more than a stereotype.

Though the inflexibility and the timidity of his class amuse Ralph,
he loves and respects the old traditions, aristocratic decor, and conservative people, and he resents the newly rich with their vulgar
ways more than he knows. In spite of his generosity and magnanimity, he has little power of self-criticism. He completely misinter-
prets, for example, his initial relationship to Undine: He sees himself
as saving her from the influence of other Invaders by enlarging her
vision, whereas it is he finally who adapts to her constricted standards and recognizes in himself, in at least latent form, those
qualities that he most hates in her. For instance, when he criticizes
her harshly for refusing to see in her pregnancy anything besides illness, anxiety, and expense, he suddenly realizes that he has himself
been harboring a similar reaction to it. Again, after appealing in vain
to her to curb her profligate spending, he recognizes that she is fundamentally more shrewd about money matters than he is and that he
resents her determined bargaining.

As Ralph knows Undine better, he moves from worship to disillusionment to forgiveness to anger and finally to despair; but he never learns to meet her on her own terms or to struggle as determinedly as she does. He despises his own inadequacy without being able to do anything about it, and he realizes with despair that his education, training, and the very traditions that have molded him prevent him from confronting with decisiveness the relentless Invaders who have taken Paul from him, as if the child were simply a possession to be bargained for. Undine's demand for custody of their son, simply to blackmail Ralph into paying her more money, exemplifies her cruelty and toughness.

Marvell's suffering invests the novel with depth and complexity, and his suicide adds to its human dimensions in its spectacle of a worthy man brought low by unforeseen, harsh, and inevitable forces. His death brings into focus the full degree of Undine's hardness and incorrigibility because she feels no remorse about the man whose death she has caused. His death is opportune since it allows her to marry as a widow rather than as a divorcée and to become wealthier through her child's inheritance. She has a vague feeling of regret, however, about the sudden solution to her problems: "She continued to wish that she could have got what she wanted without having had to pay that particular price for it" (487).

As in earlier novels, Edith Wharton uses interior decoration, paintings, books, and furnishings to establish tone and to provide insight into the characters. For instance, the Spragg suite at the Hotel Stentorian exemplifies the tastelessness and extravagance of the newly rich, but Mrs. Spragg's discomfort, as she sits like a mannikin in the midst of her lavish furnishings, indicates that she is isolated and that New Yorkers have not accepted her even with her wealth. The Spraggs's pretentious yet ugly possessions formed no part of their Midwestern lives and are no valid mirror now of their lack of taste. The newly rich simply spend lavishly, and they distrust the apparent miserliness of those who have money and do not spend it. Undine thinks it strange that the Marvells have an old-fashioned wood fire when they could afford a clean and efficient gas log or polished electric grate. Her mother suspects that the Marvells were "trying to scrimp on the ring" because Ralph presents Undine with an heirloom rather than a new ring when they become engaged. At least, the Spraggs and Moffatt are generous with what they have in contrast to the Marvells, Dagonets, and de Chelles who tend to feel that elegant manners compensate for their more furtive materialism.

Though Elmer Moffatt becomes a collector of paintings and

books, these treasures, Edith Wharton makes clear, do not reflect his taste so much as his eagerness to purchase them before other millionaires do so. Even the nine-year-old Paul has more sensitivity than do his mother and latest stepfather. He senses that the tapestries which they have bought from Raymond de Chelles belong in the drafty hall of the château, not in the Moffatt mansion, and he cries bitterly as if sensing his own isolation. He is alienated from the opulence that surrounds him as was Mrs. Spragg ten years before. The child wanders through the mansion, and, reaching out for the beautifully bound books, he finds that they are always locked up because they are too valuable to be read.

Mrs. Wharton sketches in so economically her minor characters that they remain vivid whenever they appear at intervals in this long narrative. Clare Dagonet's hypocrisy is, for example, forcefully established from the beginning. She feels that she demeaned her class by marrying a Van Degen from among the nouveau riche, but Edith Wharton lets us know that Clare "repents" while wearing the Van Degen diamonds. Clare is able to condone Van Degen's infidelity simply because he makes life easy for her. Similarly, the hypocrisy of Mrs. Marvell is established; she cannot see sexual matters clearly because she has been taught to evade such realities and is benumbed by fear of scandal. She registers shock when Undine tells her that Mabel Lipscomb may get a divorce simply to better herself socially. Yet Mrs. Marvell does not consider the people involved in a marriage or its dissolution and is content to think of a divorcée as being in the category of the unmentionable: in New York "a divorced woman is still — thank heaven — at a decided disadvantage" (95). In a character like Bertha Shallum, Edith Wharton stresses the lack of inhibition that Undine sees as admirable and Raymond de Chelles rejects as vulgar. As she prepares for a day of pleasure with Undine, Bertha begins "screaming bilingually" at successive windows in the building's long facade.

In *The Custom of the Country*, Edith Wharton conveys a sense of depth and abundance; and she reveals a sophisticated artistry and breadth of social knowledge. The most truly panoramic of her books, it is a stirring recreation of the pre-World War I milieu in America and France. Her sense of human values is strong, if somewhat deflected by her satiric impulses; and her insight into human motivation and her sense of the moral implications of her characters' decisions are firm and commanding.

CHAPTER 6

The Short Stories

I "A shaft driven straight into the heart of experience"

E DITH Wharton's artistry in the short story is subtler and
her imaginative reach greater than her own somewhat
prescriptive literary theory might lead us to expect. In *The Writing
of Fiction* (1925) she sets forth her views on the form of a good short
story by emphasizing its directness: it must not be a web loosely
drawn over many aspects of life but "a shaft driven straight into the
heart of experience." In her view, all fiction develops through the
separating of "crucial instances" from the general experience, but
the short story exacts from its author more skill in recognizing and
interpreting such moments of significance. The author must introduce no irrelevant detail to distract the reader's attention for a
moment. The effect of compactness and instantaneousness, she
thought, would result from the strict observation of the unity of time
and from the use of a single pair of eyes to focus upon the rapidly
enacted episodes. The establishing of a vital, vivid impression, she
asserted, is imperative in order to insure the reader's vicarious
presence in the milieu or his identification with the conflict
presented. The beginning of a short story, therefore, stretches a
writer's resources more than the conclusion.

For the story, even more than for the novel, the artist's selection
from his experience and his reduction of its chaotic aspects to some
sort of order are indispensable. Throughout her career, she reiterated
these two principles; and she increased her emphasis upon them as
experimental writers became fascinated with the "stream of consciousness" and as Naturalist writers became obsessed with revealing
a "slice of life." Her own stories manifest her conviction that art cannot simply reflect life; the artist must refine upon his experience by
turning his materials about and by focusing them until exactly the

right light refracts through them. Effective economy arises naturally when an author is so imbued with the subject that he feels no temptation to decorate its surface with adventitious elements which might be interesting in themselves but not crucial.

Her careful ordering of detail enabled Mrs. Wharton to attain in many of her shorter works a psychological complexity in characterization which would ordinarily be found only in the novel. In her short stories she usually illuminates, rather than resolves, the refractory situations that she subjects to her scrutiny. The characters and events often suggest intonations of the universal and ranges of significance beyond the literal. Edith Wharton's endeavor to develop exhaustively the importance of selected aspects of experience often led her beyond the short story to the novella, a form which gave freer opportunities for the revelation of character but which still imposed some limitation on the number of persons and episodes.

Characteristically, her best tales reveal extraordinary psychological and moral insight; and they achieve distinction through her exploration in them of human situations of considerable complexity. The stories often move into the realm of the symbolical and allegorical, especially in those dealing with the supernatural. Characters in all her best stories — as in her tales of the supernatural — assume archetypal dimensions, reaching toward the universal.

II *The Outpouring of Half a Century*

Altogether, Edith Wharton's short fiction includes eleven novellas and eighty-six short stories. Most of the stories, first published in magazines, were reprinted in the eleven collections that she compiled between 1899 and 1937; but the stories appeared constantly throughout her career which began in 1891. One third of them appeared before her first great novel, *The House of Mirth* (1905), and were mostly reprinted in three collections: *The Greater Inclination* (1899), *Crucial Instances* (1901), and *The Descent of Man* (1904).

These early works include efforts as distinguished and as varied in theme and tone as "A Journey," "Souls Belated," "The Mission of Jane," "The Other Two," "The Quicksand," and "The Lady's Maid's Bell." The chief characteristic marking them as early work — a tendency toward the epigrammatic — slows the pace. Dialogue is marked by virtuosity, and authorial comment calls attention to itself. These stories for the most part do not fully attain the depth and complexity of her later work. Yet the themes she most often explores in them are those that dominate her subsequent fiction: the mystery of the supernatural, the development of the artist, and the nature and role of women in society.

She finished the second third of her brief fiction by 1916 and collected it in *The Hermit and the Wild Woman* (1908), *Tales of Men and Ghosts* (1910), and *Xingu* (1916). "The Eyes," a chilling indictment of a man's sinister nature, and "Xingu," a delightfully amusing satire on intellectual pretension, represent only two of her outstanding contributions in this genre from this middle period.

The final third of her stories appeared after World War I and include many of her finest: "Miss Mary Pask," "Bewitched," "Atrophy," "A Bottle of Perrier," "After Holbein," "The Day of the Funeral," "Joy in the House," "Pomegranate Seed," and "Roman Fever." These she published in *Here and Beyond* (1926), *Certain People* (1930), *Human Nature* (1933), and *The World Over* (1936). Her last volume, *Ghosts* (1937), contained only one previously uncollected tale (the excellent "All Soul's"); and it is the only collection that contains stories of only one type and a preface by the author. Though masterful short fiction appeared in every decade of Edith Wharton's long career, she may have reached the peak of her skill in the 1920's and 1930's — a fact that argues against the assumption that her creativity waned after *The Age of Innocence* (1920).

III   *The Ambiguous Role of Woman*

In roughly thirty of her stories, as well as in several of her novels and novellas, Edith Wharton examined the role and status of women, the implications of marriage as seen through the eyes of a woman, the relationship between mother and child, and the rapidly changing views about divorce and about liaisons outside of marriage. Though she explored these subjects insistently, she approached the issues from varying angles and arrived at contradictory conclusions. If any consistent pattern of conviction emerges from the stories, which cover almost fifty years, it is that each woman must decide for herself what is best in her own situation. When Edith Wharton began writing, divorce in many parts of America spelled disgrace not only to the divorcée but to her relatives; yet divorce was commonplace only a few years later . Views on love affairs outside marriage changed much more slowly. In any event, it is remarkable that in the 1890's and even at the turn of the century a woman from Mrs. Wharton's conservative milieu could examine so vigorously and so searchingly issues related to divorce and to love, legal or illicit. Certainly no American author before 1930 produced such penetrating studies of women who, instead of marrying, decide to risk social ostracism by contracting temporary alliances based on mutual trust and sexual desire.

In other stories in this early period, Mrs. Wharton deplores the fact that women in 1900 knew little about the lives their husbands led. While she saw such sheltered existence as stultifying, she recognized that, when women gained worldly understanding, they had no power to change whatever they found amiss. Only painful disillusionment and resigned acceptance result from enlightenment, as in "The Lamp of Psyche" (1895),[1] when a woman learns that her husband had avoided military service by questionable means, and in "The Letters" (1910), when a woman discovers unopened all the love letters she had written her husband before their marriage. In both stories, the ending suggests that the husbands ironically never notice that the adoration of their wives has turned to patient forbearance.

Edith Wharton's humorous approach to divorce in "The Other Two" (1904) was remarkable for its time. She suggested varying answers to the question of the degree of choice that remains to a woman after marriage in three of her astringent tales: "Fullness of Life" (1891), "The Reckoning" (1904), and "The Quicksand" (1904). In "Souls Belated" (1899), Mrs. Wharton implied that marriage may be an artificial formality and a mere extraneous convention when love invests a liaison outside of marriage. She was still wrestling with such problems three decades later in *The Gods Arrive* (1932), a fact which suggests that the personal, psychological, and sexual problems confronting women at the turn of the century were not to be resolved in her lifetime. Later excellent stories center around these themes that R. W. B. Lewis designates collectively as "The Marriage Question."[2] They include stories such as "Autres Temps," "The Day of the Funeral," "Joy in the House," "Diagnosis," "Roman Fever," and "Pomegranate Seed."

IV *The "projection of . . . inner consciousness"*

Because Edith Wharton wrote so voluminously in the genre, I have chosen for discussion only three short stories that seem to be representative of her high achievement, particularly as she explores in them the human psyche: "The Eyes," "Bewitched," and "After Holbein." Mrs. Wharton reveals remarkable subtlety in "The Eyes"

(1910), an acute analysis of the blindness of the/esthetic temperament. She is concerned in this tale with the ramifications of Andrew
Culwin's moral deficiencies as they have undermined his own life
and the lives of others. A gracious, wealthy, cultured man, Culwin
surrounds himself with disciples. Twice, at times of self-satisfaction
when he has judged that he has acted in a kindly way, he has had a
vision of leering red eyes at night. Whether they are the result of
faulty vision, hallucination, or "a projection of my inner consciousness," the reader himself must decide. A master at self-
deception, Culwin cannot see, until the final moment in the story,
that the eyes are a symbol of his own hidden weakness. Irony derives
from his assurance, before he relates his experience to his disciples,
that he is done now and forever with the apparition, whereas he
himself becomes the apparition.

At the completion of the tale, he is amused when one of the young
men recoils from him. At last, as he looks into the mirror, he
recognizes the lurid countenance with its horrible eyes as his own.
The supernatural has, in fact, become the natural; the fearful
hallucination has become the even more terrifying actuality and
emphasizes the completeness of Culwin's degeneration. In contrast
to James's more discursive supernatural narratives, Mrs. Wharton
often made use of a single obsessive and obtrusive image to organize
a given tale. The lurid eyes are, furthermore, a compelling projection of the slightly decadent atmosphere surrounding Culwin even
in his beautiful library and of his moral occlusion: his inability to
realize that complacent non-involvement in human relationships
represents, in reality, the most despicable kind of involvement.

In "Bewitched" (1926) Mrs. Wharton analyzes psychic reactions
and uses supernatural phenomena symbolically in studying the
effects of isolation and fear in remote New England. Prudence
Rutledge alleges that her husband, Saul, has for a year been
bewitched and gradually debilitated by the ghost of a girl, Ora
Brand, in whom he had been interested before his marriage. With
quiet malignity, Mrs. Rutledge insists that a stake — undoubtedly a
phallic emblem — be driven through the breast of the dead girl to
keep her ghost from walking and to release Saul from the spell that is
compelling him to meet her spirit. Mrs. Rutledge almost certainly
thinks of her as a succubus who must afford Saul an intense, if illicit,
sexual satisfaction that contrasts with her own frigidity.

Prudence summons three neighbors to carry out her demand, one
of whom is Sylvester Brand, the widowed father of the "witch";

another, Orrin Bosworth, the recording consciousness of the story; and the third, a local ecclesiastic, Deacon Hibben. That evening the men discover a woman's footprints in the snow leading from the cemetery to the hut, which has been the trysting place. One of them fires a shot, and something white rises up in the darkness. A few days later Brand's other daughter, Venny, dies of pneumonia, and Bosworth suspects that Ora has drawn her sister to the grave in her loneliness, now that her lover has eluded her spell. Ambiguity enough remains for us to suppose that Venny may have been the "ghost," but we identify too strongly with the sensible Bosworth to accept absolutely a detached and rational explanation. The characters seldom lose control of themselves, the action is underplayed, and their control of their inner distress enables us to identify closely with them.

The effectiveness of the tale derives mostly from Mrs. Rutledge and from the imaginative intensity with which Mrs. Wharton envisioned her; the spectacle of the sinner and his punishment animates Mrs. Rutledge. For a woman who believes so compulsively the precept on her parlor wall, "The Soul that Sinneth It Shall Die," it is but a step to proclaim, "Thou shalt not suffer a witch to live." She is a blighting presence, as the references to her marblelike pallor, her white eyelids, her cold eyes "like sightless orbs" or "marble eye-balls," and her shrivelled hands indicate. Relaxed after the funeral of Venny, she remarks casually, "it sometimes seems as if we were all walking right in the Shadow of Death."

The narrator of the tale, Bosworth, provides its other chief focus, and its complexities of meaning are mostly developed through his reflections upon character and incident. Through him, Mrs. Wharton maintains the single point of view at the same time that she juxtaposes his varying depths of consciousness to achieve intense dramatic effect. Like the narrator in *Ethan Frome,* Bosworth is less provincial than the people he describes; unlike him, Bosworth is basically a Hemlock County man, whose feelings — in spite of his intellectual reservations — are rooted in generations of belief in witches and ghosts.

The effectiveness of this story also depends on Mrs. Wharton's understanding of the difficulties to be endured in New England rural life. The stoical withstanding of hardship is a measure of the strength of the characters, but their isolation makes them prey to neurotic fears. Sylvester Brand is an alienated man with the laugh of one who has never known gaiety. He works hard to no purpose on his barren

land. His wife and both daughters die young. At the funeral of Venny, his face suggests that he is now going home alone, identified only
with death: "Brand's face was the closed door of a vault, barred with
wrinkles like bands of iron." It is no accident that the story — like
another ominous tale, "The Triumph of Night," and like *Ethan
Frome* — takes place in the depth of the New England winter when
the physical landscape can reinforce the psychic tensions oppressing
the people in the community. There is no sharp line between the
normal and the abnormal psyche nor between the real and the supernatural. In the vast, remote area, covered by snow, the sharp line
between psychic dislocation and the spirit world dissolves.

In symbolic power and psychological subtlety, "After Holbein"
(1928) represents another culmination in Edith Wharton's artistry in
the short story. The decadence of an old aristocracy and the peculiar
perspective on life available to those approaching death provide its
themes; and the Holbein woodcuts of *The Dance of Death* provide
its inspiration. The protagonist, Anson Warley, is a bachelor dilet-
tante who is also an Everyman figure, confronted as all must finally
be by death. Irony suffuses his situation and generates pathos for us
as he realizes too late that he has wasted his life in incessant social
pursuits in a shallow society.

As a young man, Anson Warley had embraced standards of excellence. Evalina Jaspar, once the leading hostess of New York
society, is now senile; but she refuses to relinquish her role in it.
Almost daily she plans parties, checks guest lists, dresses in velvet
gown and jewels, dons a purplish wig, and greets imaginary guests.
Her situation supplies an antiphonal comment on Warley's; and his,
in turn, refracts and defines hers. Though Warley is ill for several
hours with ominous symptoms of an impending stroke, he finds his
way to her doorstep in formal dress. Their diminished activities this
night, in effect, caricature what had formerly been merely a
caricature of life as they participate again in the social activities of a
deadened society with its gracious rituals and irresponsible attitudes.

Death pervades the entire story which covers one day, includes
many flashbacks to the earlier lives of the two, and culminates in the
banquet scene. Just as the skeleton in the Holbein engravings summons his figures to death, Anson and Evalina are such spiritual
skeletons to each other. Each is the other's victim, perhaps, but each
is also the agent who brings the other to a confrontation of a final, inescapable reality. Because of their infirmities, which make them
perceptive at some points and unexpectedly oblivious to reality at

others, a confused dreamlike or "ghostly" atmosphere invests the story. Strange perspectives and patterns appear, as when Anson in the forenoon suffers a dizzy spell and sees the universe from a new angle as he recovers. In the final scene, imaginary guests file into Evalina's dining room; and, after this "ghostly cortège" has passed, Evalina and Anson "advance with rigid smiles and eyes straight ahead." They recognize the non-material people sitting with them at the table, and they see food and flowers not visible to the nurse and maid observing the scene "off-stage." In a parody of the Last Supper, the vintage wine is soda water, and the bread is unsavory mashed potatoes. Yet a kind of fellowship is reached, a moment of spiritual communication long absent in their lives.

Tragedy lies not in the death of the principals, since death is a fate no one evades, but in the pointless lives they have led. Excessive sympathy for the characters would have weakened the Faustian inevitability of this final scene: Anson has lost the "Alps and the cathedrals" he had once dreamed of, but he and Evalina have had the sterile satisfactions that they settled for. They have paid for their death-in-life with the death of their own souls. Both have made life itself a dance of death. "After Holbein" is a parable that signifies that the wages of wasted talent is death and that complacency may indeed be the greatest of social sins.

CHAPTER 7

The Age of Innocence

I Stability and Change:
the Novel's Significance and Structure

*T*HE *Age of Innocence* (1920) is, perhaps, Edith Wharton's masterpiece. The work of a mature artist, it represents her in a more mellow and elegiac mood than that expressed in *The House of Mirth* or in *The Custom of the Country* in which the analytical impulse had dominated. Now the element of affection for a bygone age tempered her satire; and, if her criticism of the unworldliness of her aristocrats is still sharp, she sees that they also exemplified certain humane values by which they ordered their lives. For several years Mrs. Wharton had been diverted from the writing of novels and had published only shorter fiction, as if to acknowledge that the strain of creating a large-scale work was too great when the world was convulsed by war and by the sufferings that were its aftermath. Yet with *The Age of Innocence* Mrs. Wharton wrote again a major novel which has challenged the attention ever since of readers and critics.

She controlled and articulated the action in this novel as perfectly as she had in *The House of Mirth*. Every incident and almost every remark, no matter how trivial, contribute to the central dilemma that faces Newland Archer in the book — his choice which he must make between May Welland and Ellen Olenska, a choice which he realizes later has been made for him by the society in which he grew up and by the two women who love him. The novel consists of two books of equal length; the first one moves from the engagement of Newland Archer and May Welland in January to their marriage in April, and the second recounts the first eight or nine months of their marriage.

The tension in both books arises from Archer's love for May's cousin, Ellen Olenska, who has recently arrived from Europe after fleeing an abusive, dissolute husband. More concerned for the family's reputation than for Ellen's welfare, Archer joins her aristocratic relatives in persuading her not to seek a divorce lest she bring a breath of scandal upon them all. But, in a reversal of his prior arguments, he asks her (at the end of Book I) to free herself and to marry him. Ironically, his earlier advice has been so effective that she now refuses happiness at the expense of others, particularly of May. One moment of expressed love accentuates in its intensity and poetry the suffering for both which is implied in Ellen's renunciation: "He had her in his arms, her face like a wet flower at his lips, and all their vain terrors shrivelling up like ghosts at sunrise" (170).[1]

Book II begins with the April wedding and ends the following winter when Ellen Olenska returns to Europe, though not to her husband. On the eve of Ellen's departure, May stages a farewell dinner, an event that underlines the finality of Ellen's decision to leave. Her entire "tribe" of relatives and the luminaries of society who witness this solemn ceremony thus place an irrevocable seal on her plans. Ironically, most of them think that Ellen has been Archer's mistress; but they do not admit their suspicions in anything they say or do. In their eyes, Archer and Ellen get no credit for the rectitude that has been so difficult for them to maintain.

Later, when alone with Archer, May meets his announcement that he wants to go far away with her own — that she is pregnant. The implacability of fate toward him strikes him with numbness. Romantic affection for May has trapped him, he sees with agony; and he further realizes that his own tendency to idealize women has also betrayed him. For one so constituted as he, it is impossible to disregard the expectations of his society that he will do his duty toward her. The sparseness of the words that he can speak in this scene suggests the shock which this final frustration engenders: "He looked up at her with a sick stare, and she sank down, all dew and roses" (346). With a cold hand, feeling only his own disappointment, he strokes her hair as he goes through the tender but now empty rituals of a husband and protector.

Ostensibly the novel should end here. But the single remaining chapter is integral to the total esthetic structure of the novel. Twenty-five years elapse between Archer's perfunctory embrace of May and the final chapter. She has meanwhile borne three children and died after twenty-five years of marriage in which she was "generous, faithful, unwearied." For his part, Newland has been a "good citizen." Though he acknowledges to himself that he has missed the "flower of life," he also realizes that this flower is as remote from most people as a lottery prize. With serenity he can now recall Ellen and his transcendent passion for her. He thinks of her, not so much as an actual woman, but as a figure from a book or as a woman in a picture. Finally, he also recognizes that May knew all along of his love for Ellen; and he now finds comfort in knowing that someone had guessed his secret and pitied him: "that it should have been his wife moved him indescribably." He sits for a long time across the street from Ellen Olenska's apartment building in Paris. Ultimately, he decides not to cross the street and sends his oldest son to see Ellen in his place. The world changes, and a man cannot return to the past.

If a mellowness and a tolerance which were present more by implication in Edith Wharton's earliest fiction now dominated her vision, an assuredness and authority dominated her craft. In *The Age of Innocence,* she wrote her most consistently articulated and sophisticated novel — one more perfectly wrought than her other two masterpieces in her control of subject. *The House of Mirth* and *The Custom of the Country* had tended at times to be too inclusive in scope and too encyclopedic in coverage, and she had not always been able to achieve a form that could contain the abundance of her inspiration.

When she attained classic form in *The Reef,* it was at the expense of the ultimate significance of the novel. That *The Age of Innocence* is a shorter novel than either *The Custom of the Country* or *The House of Mirth* reveals the writer's discipline and her creation of a form absolutely suitable for her subject. Seldom has her mastery of technique been equaled in a twentieth-century novel; and she reveals her abundant resources as a novelist most remarkably in marshalling the incidents of her plot, in writing dialogue with infinite nuances, in conceiving fully wrought characters, in controlling the point of view, and in maintaining a complex tone composed of irony and enthusiasm. She satirizes a society that she also respects.

In writing *The Age of Innocence,* Edith Wharton did not retreat into an ivory tower by celebrating a past culture and by focusing on technique, as some critics maintain. In a sense, she did try to escape the vexations after the war years by commemorating a culture that she had known as a child. Although she had formerly exposed this era for its destructive frivolity and triviality, she finally appreciated it for its stability, especially in view of the fact that the years succeeding it were marked by violence, flux, and dissolving standards. But the scope and complexity of the problems presented in

The Age of Innocence 95

the novel argue against those critics (even some like Stuart P. Sherman and Robert Morss Lovett who were on the committee that awarded her the Pulitzer Prize) who deplored its lack of contemporary relevance.[2] Granted that Mrs. Wharton recreated a past culture with some reverence, she also saw that culture dispassionately; and she emphasized that its prejudices and problems still confronted America fifty years later, sometimes in more pressing guise. *The Age of Innocence* reveals a universal dimension as Edith Wharton comments upon the oppression of women by convention and their emancipation from it, the role of marriage and the family in determining the quality of a civilization, and, above all, the conflict between sexual passion and moral obligation.

Vernon Parrington was typical of the earlier critics who praised Edith Wharton's artistry but criticized *The Age of Innocence* both for its alleged lack of contemporary relevance and its failure to transcend in its implications the milieu that it mirrored.[3] Such critics failed to see the connection between the New York of the 1870's and the America of the 1920's; but, as we must admit, Mrs. Wharton herself did not stress explicitly this connection. Later critics like Blake Nevius have also discounted *The Age of Innocence* because it limits itself to an atypical segment of America in the 1870's and does not reflect such American phenomena as the development of the labor movement, immigration from foreign lands, governmental corruption, the exploitation and waste of American resources, and the influence of the frontier.[4]

Surely, any facet of society, when recreated with verisimilitude and insight, adds to an understanding of human nature; and such must have been Edith Wharton's aim as a literary artist. In *The Age of Innocence* she developed the social, moral, and intellectual conflicts that had undermined the authority of the New York aristocracy in the 1870's, she mirrored their manners and conventions though she acknowledged their absurdity, she revealed a moral vision sensitive alike to the worth of tradition and the need for change, and she implied that the passing of a gracious order had its tragic as well as its inevitable aspects, much as Anton Chekhov had presented them in *The Cherry Orchard* and in other plays. We can concede to her critics that Edith Wharton in *The Age of Innocence* limited her subject, but we need not concede that it lacks significance as she developed it.

In discussing the structure of *The Age of Innocence*, Joseph Warren Beach observed that, with few exceptions, each chapter presents one scene, that each scene is pertinent to the central action, that nearly every scene has Archer as its focal presence, and that his mind interprets most of the action. Yet, for Beach, Archer himself never becomes the vital person that other characters in the novel do.[5] Yet Archer can hardly be presented as a strong and dominant character because Edith Wharton conceived him as exemplifying a group of people who deliberately limited their experience and imagination because they were inhibited by tradition and by fear of criticism from their peers. If he is not a dominating presence, he is still a pervasive one in whom the conflicts presented in her novel center. Because he grows through his love for Ellen Olenska, Edith Wharton emphasized the changes that occurred in him. The result is that the point-of-view character reveals an increasing complexity as the novel develops.

Mrs. Wharton's maintenance of the single view, however, was not rigid; she frequently compared Archer's perspective with that of May Archer or Ellen Olenska, and she necessarily supplemented his observations with authorial comment that was not limited by his unsuspected blindness to the world beyond the closed society that he knew so well. She also significantly utilized the viewpoints of secondary personages like old Catherine Mingott, Sillerton Jackson, Larry Lefferts, and Monsieur Rivière; but all of these characters are relatively uninvolved in the principal action. She stressed Archer's overt behavior and his interaction with the two women he loves, as much as she did his deepening insight and the impact that his exclusive social group and his glimpses of a freer world outside have upon him. Certainly her concern with maintaining a single point of view in this novel was less absolute than James's or her own in *The Reef*.

II   *"Invincible innocence": the Social Panorama*

The New York society of the 1870's tended to confuse a cloistered virtue with respectability and even with morality. As a constructive force, innocence, as Edith Wharton regarded it, denoted the alleged purity of those who followed a socially prescribed moral code which stressed fidelity and family loyalty in personal relationships within a restricted social class. For those who engaged in business, the code placed a commendable emphasis upon probity rather than opportunism. Admirable as it was in many respects, this code, particularly in its personal aspects, had severe limitations. It was, at bottom, dishonest. Its adherents valued superficial pleasantness rather than a disturbing reality, they condemned those who did not conform to conventional patterns or who might threaten to change these patterns, and they cherished "respectability" more than the claims of individual liberty.

In the opening scene Newland Archer finds the "innocence" of May Welland, his betrothed, appealing. When he attends the opera with her, he assumes with approval that she cannot even recognize Faust's intent to seduce Margaret. But gradually he resents the probability that she will shut herself away from life, as her mother has, by refusing to become involved in the problems of others. Placid Mrs. Welland, in her "invincible innocence," excuses herself from listening to Ellen Olenska's troubles because she must keep her mind "bright and happy" for the sake of her slightly ailing husband. Even before Newland's marriage, he realizes with a shock that he does not want May to be like her mother. He wants more than Mrs. Welland's "innocence that seals the mind against imagination and the heart against experience" (145).

Although Archer does not evince Mrs. Welland's naïveté, he never fully recognizes his own conventionality. Considering himself capable of teaching May the value of music and books, he nevertheless has little interest in learning about the great world outside his own circle; and he finds comfort in the stability of New York society. Though he believes that cultural interests such as the opera have enlarged his mind, he is so limited by exclusive traditions that he expresses relief that the opera house is too small to accommodate the newly rich. He accepts the idea that all German texts of French operas sung by Swedish performers should be translated into Italian for American audiences — just as he accepts "all the other conventions on which his life was moulded." All aspects of Archer's life fall into settled patterns, and his indecisiveness prevents him from rebelling against those forces that constrict the spontaneous expression of the self and that encourage him to overlook evils demanding rectification. His conventionality is symbolized by the routine parting of his hair with two silver-backed brushes, the flower in his lapel, and his provincial pride at being a New Yorker, though he regards himself, ironically, as cosmopolitan.

Edith Wharton revealed Archer's limited views, subtly and ironically, at the very times that he is evaluating complacently, from the heights of his presumed sophistication, the limited views of others, particularly those of May and Ellen. Charmed by Ellen Olenska's imagination and experience, he nevertheless reacts with hypocritical conservatism when he refuses to acknowledge her need to divorce a cruel, unfaithful husband. To recognize openly her bitter experience would be to acknowledge that a woman of his wife's family knows too much about sex. Archer's temptation to be unfaithful to May ultimately helps him achieve a greater honesty about himself; he is now able to recognize that passion and moral convention can sometimes be strongly at odds with each other. As a result of his admitting his own passions and his ultimate desire for an illicit affair with Ellen, he attains a degree of tolerance for those outside his own circle of complacent and morally "superior" aristocrats.

Regarding his relatives and friends as the whole world early in the book, he assumes that Ellen's naïveté prevents her from being impressed by the party that the Van der Luydens give for her. In Archer's circle, everyone recognizes that this party is the Van der Luydens' gesture of acceptance of Ellen — an acceptance reluctantly accorded by other aristocrats since she has returned to New York without her husband. As a matter of fact, Ellen's worldly knowledge makes her refuse to attach to the party the radical significance that Archer and his friends see in it. Ellen wants only to be accepted for what she is, not forgiven for something that is not her fault. Because Newland's friends still believe in the import of such social gestures, the farewell party that May gives for Ellen also assumes importance because it symbolizes for them the end of Newland's presumed affair with Ellen.

If he initially misjudges Ellen for her failure to react according to his expectations at the time of the Van der Luydens' party, he also misjudges May by viewing her as more limited than she is. Before their marriage, he simply assumes that she will never be capable of surprising him with "a new idea, a weakness, a cruelty, or an emotion." He is himself incapable at this time of recognizing her resentment of his affair with Mrs. Rushworth or her courage at suggesting that he marry his former mistress. He does not recognize the stratagems to which May resorts in order to keep him from leaving with Ellen, nor does he realize her lasting gratitude to him for giving up Ellen. His egocentric temperament, which limits his imagination, prevents him from seeing May as a woman instead of a stereotype. He never sees that what he calls "her abysmal purity" is a myth largely of his own formulation — one that underestimates her intelligence and the extent of her worldly knowledge.

Though May appears to Archer and her male contemporaries as an image of ethereal purity and as a helpless being, she is, in Mrs.

Wharton's evaluation, a woman of considerable strength. For one thing, May enjoys athletics which were at that time largely reserved for men. Twice Mrs. Wharton refers to May's big, athletic hands — when she displays her ring and later when she tries dutifully to sit by her husband and do delicate needlework with hands meant for rowing and archery. May's interest in extending their honeymoon to Italy lies largely in the additional opportunities there to walk, ride, swim, and play tennis. Her skilled performance in "a feat of strength" at the Newport Archery contest adds dimensions of competence and assurance to her character and aligns her, in both her chaste temperament and her prowess, with Diana. She also develops much resourcefulness when Ellen threatens to undermine her hold on Archer — a toughness and a tenacity of purpose which show that she is more than the clinging, helpless woman so much cherished as the New York aristocrats' ideal.

But the old ideals of these aristocrats are being threatened by a materialism represented in the novel by Julius Beaufort. As a new millionaire, he is tolerated because he has married an aristocratic woman. Ineffectual and beautiful, his wife allows him to manage all details of their lavish menage. When the public later condemns him for a speculation that causes financial loss to others, the aristocrats pity her but also censure her for looking to her family for help now that she has married outside her circle. In the epilogue, however, Beaufort is able twenty-five years later to "buy" a place in society, and his "bastard" is about to marry Archer's son without anyone's thinking twice about what would once have seemed presumptuous. If, in the victory of such parvenus, the naïveté, exclusiveness, and censoriousness of the aristocrats have weakened, the New York community is both better and worse for the change.

The aristocrat, Mrs. Manson Mingott, links the stability of her class with the vigor and independence of the *nouveau riche*. Grotesque in her obesity, she manages, nevertheless, to be both regal and human, certainly more vigorous than her peers. She values highly the family ties and the concern for integrity which she sees in the aristocrats, but she also sees through their pretenses and their concern for propriety. No one dares gossip about her, even when she associates with Catholics, entertains opera singers, marries her daughters to foreigners, and has the first French windows in New York. In taking shortcuts around wearisome conventions, she aligns herself early in the book with Julius Beaufort; and she welcomes Mrs. Lemuel Struthers, "widow of Struthers' Shoe Polish," because new blood and new money are needed in New York society. Symbolizing the most hypocritical aspects of the establishment, Sillerton Jackson and Lawrence Lefferts become censorious, unsympathetic observers of the scene around them. Old Jackson damns with innuendo; for, when he says, "Anyhow, he — eventually — married her," the pause surrounding "eventually" speaks volumes. He is uncharitable about Ellen because her mother years before had broken with custom by allowing Ellen to wear black satin at her debut. Even more offensive is young Lefferts, who is perpetually in Sillerton's company and is, if anything, still more cynical. The tight society, for which they are spokesmen, encourages slanderous gossip precisely because it embalms so perfectly its own traditions and the life histories of its members. At the same time, these two men are insensitive to the generous aspects of these same traditions.

III   *"A hieroglyphic world": Irony, Symbol, and Image*

Edith Wharton's imagery, symbolism, ironic intonations, and stylistic assuredness in *The Age of Innocence* resulted in a more perfectly wrought and modulated work than *The Custom of the Country*. Viola Hopkins notes that Edith Wharton used an ordered style in the novel to satirize the somewhat artificial order of a conventionalized society.[6] She expressed her ironic vision in a supple prose capable of a spectrum of effects that range from derision to dry but amiable comedy. She frequently employed parallel construction and the artfully balanced sentence which ends with a satirical twist: "But the Beauforts were not exactly common; some people said they were even worse" (16); "People had always been told that the house at Skuytercliff was an Italian villa. Those who had never been to Italy believed it; so did some who had" (128). Often the irony inheres in one word that is more serious — or less so — than its context, as the "mildly" in the statement describing Archer's affair with Mrs. Rushworth — her charms "had held his fancy through two mildly agitated years" (5).

Mrs. Wharton's ironic vision throughout the novel keeps the affair between Archer and Ellen from attaining proportions of high tragedy, except briefly in Archer's own mind. Frustration as much as heartbreak marks their final separation. Consequently, Mrs. Wharton envisioned most of the love scenes with a measured objectivity, aware at once of an intense seriousness in Archer's passion as well as the difficulties in the way of its consummation. An embarrassing interruption or an unconsciously comic remark or gesture characteristically deflates the romantic and glamorous aspects of this relationship; for, as Blake Nevius notes, the lovers are almost never afforded privacy in their meetings. When Archer anticipates a secret tryst in Ellen's apartment, he arrives to find the coats of several other invited guests in the hallway. At one point, on sudden impulse, he kisses her satin-slippered foot with a degree of romantic extravagance uncharacteristic of him. Later, he kisses a pink umbrella, mistakenly assuming it to be hers. On an impulse, he goes to Boston for a furtive talk with her and finds a secluded dining room, only to be joined by an entourage of school teachers. When he makes elaborate excuses to May to prepare for a business trip alone to Washington where he will be able to see Ellen, Ellen's grandmother has a stroke, she is called home, and he can only expect to pass her train going in the other direction. Even when Archer finds himself alone with Ellen in a carriage after being delegated to drive her to her stricken grandmother, he is distracted because he is making love to Ellen in a carriage that belongs to his wife.

Early in the novel Mrs. Wharton comments that the aristocrats "lived in a kind of hieroglyphic world, where the real thing was never said or done or even thought, but only represented by a set of arbitrary signs" (42). Mrs. Wharton attached many such signs to single objects which thereby acquire a ritualistic or arcane meaning. They include the restoration of position to the Beauforts that is implied by Mrs. Mingott's carriage parked outside their door; the social acceptance of Ellen implied by the white envelope handed through the door by someone who had arrived in the Van der Luydens' carriage; and the bride's collection of three dozen of everything, monogrammed, to imply that traditional expectations are being met. A ballroom in one's house is an incontrovertible symbol of status that serves to elevate one parvenu family over another: "This undoubted superiority was felt to compensate for whatever was regrettable in the Beaufort past" (16).

Objects also serve in the novel as a symbolic means of characterizing individuals. May's satin and lace wedding dress suggests both her love of the traditional and her practicality since she plans to have a gown she can wear two years. Mrs. Mingott's cream-colored house in a period of brownstones connotes her mild rebelliousness, and Ellen's peeling stucco house suggests her poverty. Ellen's black dress of fluid cut and low neckline, May's white dress undergirded with whalebone, Ellen's red roses, and May's lilies of the valley symbolize Archer's views of these women. Ellen is for him, a woman of lush sexuality; May, a woman of virginal purity.

Mrs. Wharton not only employs objects as symbols to com-

municate with the reader but also uses them as forces that control individuals in their behavior because of the symbolic import of these
objects to the individual. For example, the Welland house with its
heavy carpets, watchful servants, and stacks of invitations and cards
on a hall table exerts a tyrannizing effect upon Archer's spirit and
suggests the restrictive aspects of his culture upon him. The Welland
way of life, like a debilitating drug, makes any existence that is less
affluent and conventional seem "unreal and precarious," but the
Welland ethos, of course, is unreal in its artifice and would be
precarious except for the inherited wealth that makes it secure. Objects in his mother's home produce a similar comforting, but
anesthetizing, reaction in Archer. In her dining room, for instance,
the candlelit portraits in dark frames on dark walls suggest to him a
reverence for ancestors and a willingness only to half-see reality.

Mrs. Wharton uses entire scenes, as well as objects, with symbolic
intent. For example, the Van der Luydens' party and May's farewell
dinner both signify, as we have noted, society's pronouncements
upon Ellen's fate. Another important scene, rich in implication, occurs when Ellen endeavors to establish for Archer a philosophical
perspective about the end of their love affair. They meet for the last
time in the antiquities room of the Metropolitan Museum. The intensity of their present conflict contrasts with the passivity of the artifacts in this room — mummies, statuary, and other objects of art
and daily use — though these artifacts are also the material evidence
of human struggles that have long since transpired. Ellen, standing
before a case of such objects labelled "Use Unknown" reflects upon
the "cruel" truth that eventually nothing matters — nothing does, in
fact, matter after a few years to any human being. A museum guard,
"like a ghost stalking through a necropolis," walks down the vista of
mummies and sarcophagi and interrupts Archer when he suggests to
Ellen that they elope. Throughout this scene references to the
"Gorgon" as a reality symbol are abundant, an image discussed
below.

Another scene early in the novel achieves notable symbolic intonations, the scene wherein the Archers call on the Van der
Luydens in a kind of pilgrimage to gain help from them as the ar-
biters of their social class. The elderly Van der Luydens and their
compatriots have little vitality, and for them the ceremonious is
everything. They symbolize, in fact, the deadness of the conventions
that attempt to preserve intact the values whose efficacy has long
ago disappeared. Their door bell echoes as through a vault, a servant

appears as if awakened from the dead, the drawing room is "enshrouded," and the Van der Luyden banquets loom as funereal in Archer's memory. To him, Mrs. Van der Luyden's rosy cheeks suggest a corpse caught in a glacier and preserved for ages. The scene also conveys the exaggerated importance accorded these social leaders and the real, though irrelevant, power that they exercise. Images related to the regal dominate when Mrs. Van der Luyden, for example, smilingly approaches her husband, like Esther seeking out King Ahasuerus, to persuade him to stage a party for Ellen.

Mrs. Wharton also makes abundant use of stylistic images to intensify the effects for which she aims. Accordingly, she satirizes inflated social conventions largely by means of images associated with the tribal or the anthropological. Ellen's farewell dinner, for example, is a "tribal rally around a kinswoman about to be eliminated from the tribe" (337), the Grace Church wedding is a ritual seemingly of an ancient vintage dating "from the dawn of history," and the secrecy surrounding the wedding journey is a "sacred taboo of the prehistoric ritual" (179 - 180).

To convey her sympathy for Archer, she resorts to nightmare images, which threaten physical danger and emphasize his torturous uncertainties whenever he thinks of leaving May for Ellen. He sees himself, as Viola Hopkins indicates, "on the edge of a steep precipice about to pitch headlong into darkness" (174), as "adrift far off in the unknown" (186), as in a "black abyss . . . sinking deeper and deeper" (187), as "clinging to the edge of a sliding precipice" (254), as "having slipped through the meshes of time and space" (231), and as existing on "the edge of a vortex" (245).

Mrs. Wharton also makes striking use of the Gorgon image to intimate the uncertainties facing the lovers, their inability to confront certain kinds of reality, and their impatience to break through conventions to attain another kind of reality. In the museum sequence, Ellen asserts that she has found a kind of salvation by submitting to the Gorgon, a mythical figure who fastens the eyelids open so that one can never again rest in "blessed darkness." As a reward for facing the truth, the Gorgon dries one's tears. Ellen accordingly prevails upon Archer to return home to May and to face reality; but, until after the farewell dinner and May's announcement of her pregnancy, Archer cannot quite face the full implications of his situation.

If the scope of *The Age of Innocence* is narrower than that customarily expected in the works of Realists in the 1920's, it would be hard to find a book in which the problems of a group of people at a certain time are more carefully perceived, their manners and conventions more meticulously documented and criticized, the tenuous balance between the values of innocence and of experience more tolerantly analyzed, and the conflicts between tradition and change more memorably dramatized.

CHAPTER 8

Three Novels of the 1920's

I An Overview of the Career after 1920: a Refusal to Stop Growing

IN an assessment of Edith Wharton's work, her last half dozen novels demand more critical attention than they have characteristically received. Some of them indicate her interest in evolving new techniques for the writing of fiction and all exhibit her continued ability to confront, with a varying degree of success, new and challenging social issues and artistic problems. In the 1920's and 1930's, as we have already seen in Chapter 6, she produced excellent works in short fiction; and she published a third of her short stories and *Old New York* (1924), which contained her last four novellas. During these late years she also wrote a volume of criticism, *The Writing of Fiction* (1925); her autobiography, *A Backward Glance* (1934); and numerous critical articles. But most important are her six novels: *A Son at the Front* (1922), *Twilight Sleep* (1927), *The Children* (1928), *Hudson River Bracketed* (1929), *The Gods Arrive* (1932), and *The Buccaneers* (1938). Two relatively inconsequential books, *Glimpses of the Moon* (1922) and *The Mother's Recompense* (1925), produced early in the period and overemphasized in discussions that alleged her artistic decline, considerably damaged her reputation with later readers and critics.

She had begun *A Son at the Front* (1922) before her greater success, *The Age of Innocence* (1920). Unfortunately, the fact that she did not complete it until 1922 colored the critical fortunes of this book. It is a better book than most commentators have conceded it to be. By the time it appeared, readers and critics were trying to forget the war; and patriotism had lost appeal, even respectability as a subject for fiction. In *Twilight Sleep* (1927) and *The Children* (1928), she was less restrained than she had previously been in writing the

comedy of manners and was also more broadly satiric. She wrote
about the deficiencies and absurdities to be found in contemporary
upper-class families, with the result that there is hardly anything of
the elegiac communication of a lost way of life, a note that had been
insistent in *The Age of Innocence.*

Hudson River Bracketed (1929), which traces the life of an artist,
though complete in itself, must be considered in relation to its se-
quel, *The Gods Arrive* (1932). In both books Mrs. Wharton analyzed
the vexatious problems that an artist must face in a materialistic and
Philistine society, and the typical sexual choice that he must make to
find emotional fulfillment in marriage or outside it. In her un-
finished novel, *The Buccaneers* (1938), she returned to the New York
past that had always haunted her imagination but which she had not
written about in a novel since *The Age of Innocence.* The fragment
reveals not only a high level of artistry but an Edith Wharton in a
more mellow, gracious, and hopeful mood than in most of her other
late works.

Like Henry James, whose overriding concern in his last novels was
with form, Edith Wharton experimented in her late career with a
variety of contemporary characters and situations; and she extended
her comic and satiric range to a use of overstatement and flamboyant
mockery beyond that found in *The Custom of the Country* and her
most stylized short stories. To the end, she reflected in her fiction a
vigorous interest in contemporary American life, which she saw with
incisiveness and sympathy. Until her death, she continued to write
about the themes that had already absorbed her: the artist's
relationship to the marketplace; the relation of a man's art to his personal life; the effect upon the individual of changing attitudes
toward marriage, sex, and divorce; and the centrifugal effects of the
modern economy upon the family.

But Mrs. Wharton's new concerns were also evident in these late
works when she wrote sympathetically, yet critically, about the
alienation and frustrations of men and women in an impersonalized
and rootless postwar era. Her concern with the isolation of people in
all age groups — with the gulf in understanding between generations, and with the relationships between parents and children —
became more insistent. She developed an overriding interest in the
relationship of her characters to a formless and shapeless social
milieu. The "tribal ceremonies" of the old New Yorkers in *The Age
of Innocence* could no longer lend pattern to the lives of those in the
postwar era. Banal substitutes for the lost values emerged in the ex-

aggerated involvement of her characters with committees, the ladies' culture club, the religious cult, and the bohemian gatherings of artists at certain cafés. Unfortunately, the causes espoused by these groups are often meaningless enterprises at best and fraudulent schemes at worst, and superficial involvement in them simply disguises the basic aimlessness of those who participate. If marital loyalties imprisoned a responsible person for life in *The Age of Innocence*, divorce and free love do not liberate, so much as complicate, lives in the later books as ex-spouses and stepparents multiply. More than ever, Mrs. Wharton emphasized the need for sharpened awareness in her personae; but, ironically, the pressures of the age deadened sensibility instead of shaping it.

The author rated her late fiction more highly than did her critics, many of whom found in it inadequate technical resources, an uninteresting version of experience, and an inability to reflect with veracity the conditions of contemporary life. When in 1936 she named her favorite works, she included, in addition to *The Custom of the Country* and *Summer*, her last three complete novels, *The Children, Hudson River Bracketed*, and *The Gods Arrive*.[1] That she did not, in her fiction of the late 1920's and 1930's, attempt to duplicate her earlier successes disappointed many. Although none of these novels is among her masterpieces, the new directions that she explored in them gave them stature, interest, importance, and some degree of lasting worth and influence.

A study of these six late novels, along with the abundant shorter fiction produced at this time, should correct such misconceptions about Edith Wharton's career as those that indicated that she had lost her artistic skill, that she had lost touch with the modern world, that she no longer understood America because she had so long been an expatriate, and that she did not understand the younger generation. In all of her late novels, she used the contemporary scene, except for *The Buccaneers;* in all six, she created sympathetically her youthful characters; and in all of them she confronted, through her central figures, the problems arising from the conflicts between generations. Even though *The Buccaneers* is laid in an earlier time, it presents social change positively.

II *The Realist's Reaffirmation: "plunging both
hands into the motley welter"*

Although Mrs. Wharton was not greatly enthusiastic about some trends in writing and in literary criticism, she nevertheless continued to be interested in contemporary literature and to have an affinity toward some younger writers. In *The Writing of Fiction*, her aim, she said, is to help new writers — not to defend her own views about literature. She wrote graciously in 1925 to F. Scott Fitzgerald after he had sent her a copy of *The Great Gatsby* with a friendly dedication, and she told him that his gesture had touched her and that she would send her latest book to him in return, "in a spirit of sincere deprecation." She assured him that he, in his novel, took a great leap beyond his earlier work; and she took time to praise several separate scenes and characters which "augur still greater things."[2] Sinclair Lewis acknowledged her as an inspiration for his work by dedicating *Babbitt* to her in 1922.

Percy Lubbock suggested that Mrs. Wharton maintained a surprising number of contacts with young Americans in the later years of her life. With these young people, Edith Wharton's shyness vanished; and she enabled them to overcome any shyness in approaching her. Lubbock described the encounters as "fun" for both her and her guests: "There was a quick light of amusement and understanding, as though she knew where she was . . . needing no introduction . . . all was well, and they could talk — and talk they must. . . . A delightful sight, and always delightful because there was no false touch in it whatever — none of patronage, none of condescension, none of benevolent superiority, least of all of any strain for an effect. She was equal in the fun."[3]

Edith Wharton's views about literature set her apart from the literary trends gaining prominence in the 1920's and 1930's, sometimes, it must be admitted, to the detriment of her work. She did not endorse such innovations in technique and subject as stream-of-consciousness, which she associated with the imitators of James Joyce, nor the explicit treatment of sex, which in her view disregarded subtleties and sensitivity and which she associated with D. H. Lawrence and James Joyce. She also rejected the use of Naturalistic or "slice-of-life" techniques, which often, in the interest of presenting a reportorial kind of social actuality, stripped man of his potential dignity as a human being and revealed him as a passive victim of deterministic natural law. Also uncongenial to her was the sociologically oriented art that dominated much of the fiction in the 1930's after the onset of the Great Depression. She recognized, however, the need to adapt conventional methods to suggest in fiction the turbulence and spiritual malaise of modern society; and, to some extent, she responded in her novels of the 1920's and 1930's by employing a more rapid shifting of scene and point of view and a more explicit treatment of social, intellectual, and sexual issues in them. But she continued to emphasize firmly, as the keystone of fiction, the need for selection of detail, for an ordered and sequential structure, and for definiteness and progression in the revelation of characters.

The writer, she thought, should check any tendency to react negatively to the accelerating changes in society after the war. Instead, he must recognize that any attempt to deny the realities of the life that surrounded him would be stultifying, ultimately, to his art. For better or for worse, he has to work with the society of which he is a part, even when he finds his milieu distasteful. In an article, "The Great American Novel," in 1927 she defined the artist's responsibility as she saw it and urged him to come to terms with the new society that had emerged from the war. For her, this society was "ephemeral, shifting, but infinitely curious to study"; and American writers, she thought, had largely passed it by in their interest in experiment and in such modern thinkers as Freud and Marx: "It is useless, at least for the story teller, to deplore what the new order of things has wiped out, vain to shudder at what it is creating; there it is, whether for better or worse, and the American novelist . . . can best use his opportunity by plunging both hands into the motley welter."[4] So spoke Edith Wharton who was the artist and the Realist to the end of her life.

III A Son at the Front *(1922)*

A Son at the Front (1922) rises above Edith Wharton's other writings about the war in its candor — in her recognition in particular that selfishness tempers most patriotism. The novel is not concerned with heroism on the battlefield so much as with the conflict between courage and fear, whether justifiable or not, experienced by those on the home front. The writer scrutinizes, on the one hand, their selfish and narrow lives; on the other, their grief and bereavements, which they face with endurance, if not always with dignity.

The "son at the front" is George Campton, whose artist-father, John Campton, and whose mother and stepfather, Julia and Anderson Brant, are wealthy American expatriates living in France. John Campton, a successful American artist who has lived long in Paris, has owed, at least in his view, part of his success to the freedom that accrued to him when he secured a divorce from his wife, Julia. Wife and child, he had assumed, could only burden him and prevent his true development as a sensibility and as a craftsman. He has recently developed, however, a strong attachment to his son, George — an attachment that suggests feelings of guilt about his long neglect of his son. When George's mother became the wife of Anderson Brant, a wealthy Parisian banker, he became attached to George by living with him as the child grew up and by supervising his education.

Edith Wharton sympathetically presented the activities of all three parents as they diligently try, throughout the early part of the novel, to keep George from being conscripted and then from being sent to the front. His own decision to volunteer for service at the battle front is apparently the result of an impulse, and his decision baffles the reader as much as it does his parents since his mood and his personality, as Mrs. Wharton presented them early in the book, do not provide the motivation for such radical action. Heretofore, his patriotism had been low-key, to say the least.

Actually, George figures in few scenes in the book; he is talked about more than he is seen. He refuses to continue his relationship with his longtime mistress after she has indicated her unwillingness to divorce her husband and marry him. Again, the motivation for George's action is baffling to his mistress and to his father, stepfather, and mother; and the motivation in terms of his function in the novel is again nebulous. George somehow thinks it more responsible to leave his beloved a widow, should he die at the front. He is wounded, recovers, returns to the front, and is killed; but his tale is not at an end. It continues with the grief of his relatives and with the relief they all feel when the Americans finally arrive to avenge not only the outrages perpetrated upon France but the death of the young man they have all loved.

Mrs. Wharton's hardly disguised, chauvinistic pro-French, anti-German bias and the depression that the characters express over America's delayed entry into the conflict tend to limit the universality of the novel. In simply dismissing this book, however, along with the other books that she produced about the war (*Fighting France*, 1915; *The Book of the Homeless*, 1916; *The Marne*, 1918; and *French Ways and Their Meaning*, 1919), critics have also overlooked Edith Wharton's satiric aplomb in this novel and her genuine creative involvement with her subject. In *A Son at the Front*, her satire constantly relates to the main action of the book and establishes its mordant, sardonic tone. Previously, in both *The Marne* and *Fighting France*, Mrs. Wharton had briefly chided flamboyant patriots who enjoyed the drama of the war — those whose patriotism had to be "fed on pictures of little girls singing the Marseillaise in Alsatian headdresses and old men with operatic waistcoats tottering forward to kiss the flag" (204).[5] This line of attack is developed further in *A Son at the Front,* because she is critical of the self-serving motives of many of her bored and restless characters who find fulfillment for their empty natures through the war. In this period, Mrs. Wharton's short stories and her *Twilight Sleep* are also critical of those Americans who pursue aimless lives, align themselves insincerely with various causes, or devote themselves to passing enthusiasms. The touch of cynicism that links *A Son at the Front* to the satires that follow it in Edith Wharton's canon not only lends distinction to the book but also saves it from the sentimentality and the propagandism that some commentators have found in it.

Mrs. Wharton is sensitive everywhere in her presentation of wartime French society to the subtle hypocrisy underlying the behavior of those at home. After George is at the front, Julia Brant finds pleasure in dropping the phrase, "my son at the front," but she finds her role as mother of a potential hero unnatural. In a storm of activity, she stages public bridge parties in her mansion to raise money for war-relief, and she surrenders her drawing room to lectures about German atrocities. In an effective satiric scene, Harvey Mayhew, an American delegate to The Hague who was appalled during a brief detention in a German jail at being accosted by prostitutes, lectures in Mrs. Brant's drawing room to the accompaniment of stirring martial music. When he is interrupted by the receipt of a telegram indicating that his nephew is missing in action, he collapses, and reality forcibly erases the sham. He has enjoyed rallying war enthusiasm, but he cannot face the cost of war to himself as an individual. In the same scene, Edith Wharton satirized even more sharply those parents who openly grieve with a bereaved individual but who secretly rejoice that they themselves have been spared such news.

In this novel Edith Wharton engendered such intensity of atmosphere and utilized such an extensive range of incisive detail that she gradually conveyed the impression of a world completely dedicated to war. The immediacy of the mobilization, the fundraising rallies, and the efforts to draw America into the war become stirring realities even while Mrs. Wharton continued her paced narrative of events. The characters, no matter how frivolous or superficial, cannot evade the agony that results from the war when personal loss is all but universal. The totality of such suffering is overwhelming; and, to her credit as artist, Mrs. Wharton consummately re-created the tragic impact of a worldwide cataclysm as it affected a group of people whose affluence and social prestige had previously protected them from the unpleasant and the violent. In her novel, people suffer so much that they can see nothing beyond war and nothing unrelated to war. She communicated the magnitude of the debacle by multiplying incidents for a cumulative effect: telegrams arrive with every post to announce another casualty until it seems as if everyone must have received at least one. In producing this pervasive sense of a world convulsed by war, of a world driven apart by the opportunism of the few and the grief of the many, Edith Wharton gave the book a timeless significance.

In this impressive panorama of all-encompassing war, she unfortunately minimized its psychological impact on her characters. They are not fully developed as individuals, yet their fates are challenging and distinctive simply as people who happen to live in a time of crisis. But the novel fails to achieve the highest excellence because Mrs. Wharton lacked her usual ability to objectify her characters — to make them more important than the milieu against which they are posed and to individualize them. Her artistry moves us to grieve for those who die and for those who mourn, but we do not often know who these people are as we do those in her other novels.

A profusion of potentially strong characters promises amplitude for the novel, but they drift away before they can make any durable impression. Adele Anthony, who came to Paris to help her alcoholic brother, became a sculptor. She stayed there for another generation after her brother was "shipped home", but she functions only as a confidante for both George and John Campton and as one more volunteer for charitable work. Madge Talkett, George's mistress, disappointingly fades out of the novel. All the characters who touch the artist's life become noteworthy, not for their relationship to him, but only for their relationship to the war; and failing to become sharply demarcated persons, they recede into the background. However, this muting of the personal may have been by design, since war allows no individual to be important. The war dwarfs the characters to the detriment of A Son at the Front as a psychological testament but to its credit as a remarkable re-creation of a world that has lost its moorings.

This novel ultimately fails of greatness since the individual characters do not develop to the extent that they could even within the confines of the milieu that Edith Wharton created for them. Most of her people illustrate something that she wished to assert about the war; and, when they served her purpose, she dropped them. Thus, Paul Dastrey loses his only son, as does George's physician; Madame Lobel, John Campton's concièrge, grieves over the death of one grandson after another; Boylston, George's college friend who visits John, founds a charity for the families of artists who are in the military or are killed; Benny Upsher, an American who makes incredible efforts to get into the French army, is killed; Davril, who aspires only to paint like John Campton, dies just before the artist can reassure him that he has talent; Madame de Dometch mourns the death of her unscrupulous lover — his death in war is much more significant than anything in his life; and Madam Olida, the fortune-teller who has comforted Julia Brant with news of George from the spirit world, ironically begs Campton to use his influence to get news of her own son at the front.

Mrs. Wharton succeeded to some extent in developing the relationships between George Campton and his artist-father, his stepfather, and his mother. She did not, however, adequately exploit either the complicated relationship between John Campton and Anderson Brant or their rivalry for the possession of George's affections. John Campton resents the years that he has missed in his son's life by deserting his family, but he tends irrationally to blame Brant rather than himself for his situation. He domineers over the self-deprecatory Anderson Brant as if to prove that the artist surpasses the businessman and that the father outranks the stepfather. The situation of the two men is close and filled with dramatic tension that seldom can be expressed; it is a highly suggestive situation even if it is not explored to the depth we expect in Mrs. Wharton's work.

John Campton must humble himself to enlist Brant's aid in getting George assigned to a safe job in the army; and the two men must, in enforced intimacy, travel together in Brant's fine automobile to the front lines where George lies severely wounded in a field hospital. Later, they try together to understand George's secret love affair with Madge Talkett. Finally, several months after George's death, John Campton manages to overcome his resentment of Brant and his money to the extent that he consents to fashion a monument for George's grave from marble paid for by the stepfather who is grieving as desperately as he for the same son lost at the front.

That the two parents, mourning inconsolably, are the father and the stepfather — rather than the estranged father and mother joined in grief — adds a memorable psychological dimension to the novel; but it is an aspect that Mrs. Wharton did not fully analyze. Julia Brant appears after George's death only as Campton thinks back about the funeral. He remembers being struck with the "perversity of attention" when he finds himself thinking of Julia's blue-red, unpowdered nose under her heavy veil at the funeral, instead of thinking about the coffin, draped with flags and flanked by glittering candles, which seems remote from him though it is only a few feet away. He pities Julia more than he does anyone else, seeing her as an "empty-hearted old woman" and knowing she will feel more isolated when she realizes how much more Brant loved George than she did and how much more he is suffering from his death. Curiously, Campton pities his former wife because he knows she will now have to fill her life with more bridge parties because her husband will be occupied with his grief for her son.

A Son at the Front deserves more recognition than Frederick J. Hoffman, for example, accorded it when he lumped it with the fiction that Dorothy Canfield and Willa Cather wrote about the war.[6] He viewed A Son at the Front, like Canfield's The Deepening Stream (1930) and Cather's One of Ours (1922), as a novel by an older-generation woman who could not, as a noncombatant, know the war firsthand as younger participants in it, like Ernest Hemingway and John Dos Passos, could. A Son at the Front is not a battlefield novel, however; it is a novel depicting the social stresses and strains that the war entailed among the civilian populace as a whole. For what she did, the novel is authentic enough; and it stemmed from the author's firsthand experience as a wartime administrator and Allied sympathizer. Outrage, which finds its vent in satire, and sympathy, which finds its expression in compassion, determined the quality of her by-no-means-negligible war novel.

IV A Modern Comedy of Manners:
Twilight Sleep

In Twilight Sleep (1927), as in The Children (1928), Edith Wharton directed her satire toward restless Americans of the 1920's. She creates in these novels situations revealing the same understanding of the ways of the rich just before the crash of 1929 that characterized her earlier satires of the decadent aristocrats and the newly rich of old New York. In both Twilight Sleep and The Children, individuals of integrity and potential find themselves caught in a dehumanizing milieu. Edmund Wilson, among the first to recognize Mrs. Wharton's work written in a new satiric mode, viewed *Twilight Sleep* as an acute work of social criticism in which she had renewed her talent with the new age.[7] In this novel, he asserted, she interpreted the modern city with great intelligence. Actually, she was less involved with the city than with the modern family for whom wealth intensifies boredom and alienation. "Twilight sleep," the anesthesia used widely in the 1920's, especially in childbirth, symbolizes in the novel the attempts made by many in the postwar decade to escape reality, either through excessive and meaningless activity or through indolence and malaise.

Edith Wharton adds perspective to the action by developing the novel through the consciousness of three different members of the family, none of whom understands the other two. Adroitly, but pointedly, she shifts the point of view among the three: Nona Manford, a sensible and sensitive young woman, who serves as the author's voice; Pauline Manford, her mother, who is excessively efficient, strenuously interested in causes and cults, and distressed at her family's separation from her (although she expects her children to schedule appointments with her through her secretary); and Dexter Manford, who married Pauline hoping that she would read aloud to him in the evenings while he reviews law cases in a corner of his mind. Instead, Dexter has found himself the victim of Pauline's perpetual campaign to keep him vigorous through involvement in social and cultural projects. He now discovers, moreover, that he is in love with Lita Wyant, the "flapper" wife of his stepson, Jim, who is a minor character but who is admirable in his love for his and Lita's child. Jim Wyant, is, in fact, a casualty of his selfish wife and of the society that countenances her, that has produced her ennui, and for which she is the spokesman. With comic perversity, Dexter daydreams of his ideal woman, who is far different from either Pauline or Lita: the pioneer woman digging potatoes in Minnesota.

Edith Wharton's secondary characters in this novel demonstrate her versatility in creating the flat personages who are effective in a stylized comedy of manners. Arthur Wyant, Pauline's ex-husband, is a gentle aristocrat who has become an alcoholic; Lita Wyant, who is bored with her husband and baby, plans to escape to Hollywood stardom; and Aggie Heuston, a lay-nun, is the frigid wife of Stanley, the man whom Nona loves passionately and hopelessly. But, motivated by a stern puritanical code, Aggie refuses to divorce her husband, Stanley, because she sees passion as a danger from which she can "save" him. Her attempt to deny the importance of sex is just as much a form of "twilight sleep," in Edith Wharton's view, as Dexter's evasion of reality and his refusal to recognize his wife as a human being and his marriage as a human responsibility.

The disaster, toward which the whole novel builds, strikes at the Manfords' elaborate country home when shots ring out after midnight; but the disaster is as much an illusion as the other aspects of the lives of these aristocrats. Pauline rushes into Lita's bedroom to discover that Arthur Wyant, in a dispute with Nona, has accidentally shot her. Nona had been trying to prevent him from killing her father, Dexter, who has been for some time with Lita in her bedroom during the absence of her husband, Jim, who is still in New York. Fortunately, Nona suffers only a surface wound and retires a few weeks later to rural solitude to regain her emotional equilibrium.

The events after the shooting are sardonically comic and only incidentally tragic in their implications. In tragi-comic confusion, the servants and the village fire department dramatically converge upon the bedroom. In the morning, the night of terror and humiliation has vanished like an hallucination induced by "twilight sleep." The participants hasten to deny the actualities of the situation and to present a doctored version of events to the public. These social leaders, incapable of facing the implications of what they have done, cannot inform the public of the truth. The butler has notified the police that a window was forced, and the morning papers accordingly already report that a burglar fired the shots. The family members depart discreetly for Canada or Europe until they can return to New York with impunity, resume their careless lives where they have left them, and subject themselves again to the unrealities induced by "twilight sleep."

The principal crux in criticism of this novel is the moral and esthetic adequacy of this climactic shooting scene. Is it adequate for the novel? Is it an adequate expression of Mrs. Wharton's satiric propensities? Edmund Wilson, otherwise a strong advocate of the book, alleged that the disaster is not significant enough in itself to serve as the catastrophe toward which the whole novel builds.[8] This scene is more adroit and more organic to the novel, however, than even Wilson allows. Though Nona is the only one to suffer intensely, her suffering is genuine. She recoils from the concept of a loveless marriage which her mother advocates for her and the spurious loyalties implied in it. She also feels revulsion toward the hypocrisy of a society that hastens to deny realities such as treachery, adultery, and attempted murder in an effort to keep the surfaces of life pleasant and serene. Yet Nona does love these people whom she can't respect; and her retreat from society, we infer, will be only temporary.

If *Twilight Sleep* were designed as high tragedy, we might agree with Wilson that the climactic scene lacks impact and pertinence. But Mrs. Wharton did exactly right to end her novel with a ruthless exposé of the moral weakness of her central figures. If they were sensitive and self-conscious, the catastrophe would, of course, drastically affect them. But Edith Wharton's point is precisely that insensitivity so completely encloses the modern rich that they cannot even recognize the scathing fires through which they walk. They are incapable of conceiving any conflict between morality and desire, they are impervious to the suffering of others, and they are unable to distinguish between the trivial and the notable. Even the cataclysm that they bring upon themselves is not recognized as a cataclysm; and something that more ordinary people would recognize as horrible they shrug off and cover up. "Twilight sleep" — the escape from pain and responsibility — is what they all want. They are inherently unsympathetic — they have been dehumanized.

Among the characters, only Nona Manford rises above the spiritual limitations of her peers. She suffers in the brief climax of the novel with its threat of multiple murders because she refuses the anodyne of pleasure and irresponsibility which her world so freely offers. Rather, she experiences to the full a sense of outrage to her moral sensibilities as she acknowledges her peers for what they are. Still, she is able to sympathize with them in their futile suffering even when they do not themselves realize that they are suffering; and, like a prophetess, she feels disaster closing in upon them all. When the catastrophe occurs, she alone cannot escape its consequences; her imaginative identification with all her friends and relatives involved in it paralyzes her spirit for a time; and she insists on going alone to the country to restore herself. Yet we must recognize that Nona's own sufferings and her satisfactions — her ability to appreciate nature, for instance — derive from an identical source — her full responsiveness to the life around her. Among the characters in the novel, only Nona, longing for the ideal, courageously confronts the real. She allows herself to love people, even though she knows they will fail her; and she achieves some of the self-knowledge that is indispensable for spiritual insight and for a true appraisal of her circumstances.

Nearly all the characters, except Nona, seek escape from boredom through excessive but aimless activity. Such escape activity is symbolized in Lita's orgiastic nude dances on the lawn of the estate of a "prophet" and in Pauline's recourse to an ultra-modern fire engine, bought as a civic-improvement project and complete with a nerve-blasting siren, to liven up her dinner party or to cover up an attempted murder. Whereas Nona responds to the beauty of a walk through the garden and the woods, her mother drives past her plantings quickly admiring only her own efficiency: "Seventy-five thousand bulbs this year. . . . It was exhilarating to be always enlarging and improving . . . to face unexpected demands with promptness and energy" (253).[9]

The aspect of modern life that Edith Wharton most saliently satirized in this novel is the attempt of the many to escape full knowledge and objective recognition of the world as it is. Hence the irony in the cliché, which literary critics and historians circulated even before she died, that she herself sought in her life and writing in her late years to escape from the realities of contemporary life. She may have wished to escape its deadening and distracting aspects, but she certainly knew, with an insider's knowledge, what it was she wished to avoid.

This novel presents best the uninhibited humor that Edith Wharton allowed herself in her late novels, for instances of her increasingly broad and earthy humor abound in it. When Pauline, for example, addresses with exaggerated assurance the Birth Control League, she discovers that, because of a mistake in her appointment schedule, she is actually standing before the Mother's Day Committee. With imperturbable command and with almost admirable resourcefulness, she changes directions and adapts her planned remarks about contraception and the overworked mothers of large families to her "new" audience. Just as she reaches the edge of the abyss, she draws a quick breath and proceeds with, "That's what our *antagonists* say — the women who are afraid to be mothers, ashamed to be mothers, the women who put their . . . convenience . . . before the mysterious heaven-sent joy, the glorious privilege, of bringing children into the world" (113).[10] She has avoided the dramatic closing remarks, planned for the Birth Control League, which refer to the vain sacrifices of mothers when illness claims the lives of the children they have borne. She donates money to an author because she finds one of his recent titles, *Beyond God,* "forward-looking," without realizing how patronizing and banal her own sentiments are.

In a description of the bungalows on the East River envisioned as a Viking-American settlement, Mrs. Wharton lampooned the fad for cheap historical reproductions. To make her Viking home "authentic," Lita's aunt spends four years in research determining what kind of rushes the ancient explorers used for covering their floors; she will wait another fifty years to have the grasses woven in Abyssinia; and she refuses to own a clock lest she introduce an anachronism into her Viking abode.

If Mrs. Wharton satirized the bogus quest for seeming authenticity, she also satirized the use of art as an escape from actuality. A bohemian friend of Lita's, to whom the real is "as tiresome as a truthful person," covers a window that provides a beautiful night-view of the Brooklyn Bridge with his picture of a brick wall and a fire escape. To such modernists, art must substitute for the real, not merely interpret it; and the substitute which they offer springs from no creative depths in the artist. In *Twilight Sleep* and *The Children*, the comic devices, outrageous and farcical as they often are, intensify Mrs. Wharton's acrid sense of the triviality of her characters. Mordant satire, not effervescent comedy, is, in reality, her mode of writing in these two novels.

Because of Mrs. Wharton's control of multiple ironies in *Twilight Sleep*, Q. D. Leavis links the novel with Aldous Huxley's extravaganzas, such as *Antic Hay, Chrome Yellow, Point Counter-Point*, and *Brave New World;* and she contends that *Twilight Sleep* compares favorably with them.[11] She also believes that all of Mrs. Wharton's satires, because they dramatize the lives of "rootless" people, provide an indispensable basis for understanding the fiction of such young writers in the 1920's as F. Scott Fitzgerald, William Faulkner, and Kay Boyle who also explored the directionless lives of their contemporaries. Mrs. Leavis's judgment about Mrs. Wharton's insight into the fruitless lives of the rich also applies to her next novel, *The Children*, which appeared the year after *Twilight Sleep*.

V The Children: *Another Tragi-comedy of Manners*

The Children (1928) centers around the struggles of the seven Wheater children to stay together after their much-divorced parents and stepparents have shunted them from one household to another. The incongruities that develop between the innocence of the children and their poisoned experience becomes Mrs. Wharton's principal theme. Fifteen-year-old Judith Wheater, who "mothers" the children, displays cynical sophistication about marriage,

adultery, alimony, and custody suits; but she remains a child in her
illiterate spelling, her love of games, and her pleasure in surprises
and trivial gifts. The adults swim, drink, and gamble on the Riviera.
While a lesser writer might have surrounded them with glamor and
excitement, Edith Wharton recognizes that in their elaborate and
anxious attempts to escape boredom, the extremely rich are apt to be
quarrelsome and dull. These adults, in an ironic sense, may also be
considered "the children" in the title of the novel.

But some adults in this world attain awareness and responsibility.
Martin Boyne, for example, develops affection for the Wheater
children after a chance encounter with them on board ship. Before
many weeks he finds himself the guardian of the children, who are
fighting to remain together without parental supervision; and he has
lost enthusiasm for his approaching marriage to Rose Sellars, a
beautiful and affluent widow. Though he is a sensitive and perceptive man, his perceptiveness does not always include knowledge of
his own emotions and motives. The women in the novel, Judith
Wheater and Rose Sellars, have more awareness concerning human
relationships than he has; and each likes to show that she is wiser
about the other than Boyne is. Hostility toward each other and a
kind of fascination with each other as the scarcely admitted rivals for
Boyne's attention motivate the two women, one only fifteen and one
middle-aged. Eventually Boyne must be convinced — by Rose
Sellars herself — that he has unconsciously fallen in love with Judith.
When he proposes to her, Judith assumes that he is teasing and
laughs like a child at the idea of marriage. His ego is so bruised by
these encounters that he leaves both Mrs. Sellars and the children in
order to live in Brazil. In a melancholy epilogue, he returns three
years later, learns of the death of one of the children, and watches
Judith dancing with a young man with whom she is evidently in
love.

Mrs. Wharton views her protagonist sympathetically, but he is not
so self-assured as the bachelors of her fiction usually are. Though he
is personable, he is something of an innocent like the children for
whom he develops such fondness. For example, he selects flamboyant jewelry for Rose Sellars, a woman of conservative and
sophisticated taste: he has little sense of what is socially fitting. He is
catapulted by his impulsiveness, his strong emotions, and his
characteristic kindness into situations where his good intentions
cause him to appear foolish. He becomes, at points, a ridiculous man
whose frustrations seem as comic to the spectator as they must be

frustrating to him. For example, when he goes to Lido to contend with the parents and stepparents (some eight or ten) who plan to separate the children, he cannot even get them all together long enough to talk; and the rapid sequence of scenes yields farcical effects. Once he corners nearly all of them in a hotel lobby; another time, in a tent on the beach. Finally — to his astonishment — they unanimously name him guardian just so that they can all run down the beach, like the larger children that they themselves are, to watch a race.

Much of the humor related to Boyne arises from the contradiction existing between his own image as a heroic figure and the petty actualities that defeat him. He has an almost Byronic conception of his own emotional potential, but the responses of others to his pretentions always disappoint him. He himself feels that the fates conspire against him to prevent the right opportunity for him to express his "greatness." Ironically, he does not realize that it is not his image as a flamboyant personality but his good nature and genuine sympathy that are admirable and that awaken the genuine responses of others. Something of a romantic dreamer about himself, he would, he is certain, be able to savor fully the people and the situations about which he has fantasized were they to become actualities: "No tremor of thought or emotion would . . . have escaped Martin Boyne; he would have burst all the grapes against his palate" (2).[12]

Instead, except for the lovely Rose Sellars whom Boyne never understands, he attracts only dull acquaintances, because he is dull without ever knowing it. In his travels he becomes intimate with assorted types of people whom he really detests. Among the grotesques are an earnest lady in spectacles who is studying the background of Sicily before going there; an elderly man who each morning announces that he gets better bacon on board ship than he could possibly get at home; and a clergyman who — though his flock has paid for his vacation trip — plans not to visit the catacombs precisely because he is expected to do so (18). The humor inherent in Martin Boyne succeeds partly because Mrs. Wharton liked him so much and was indulgent to him and partly because she caught a genuine comic type in him. The comedy in which he figures is sparked by his blunders, near-misses, mishaps, and discomfitures — all the result of his good intentions which go wrong and leave him baffled.

The humorous effects that she attempted in the children are often brilliant but sometimes strained, especially those that result from their dialogue which is at times inappropriate even for the stylized fiction with which she was experimenting. On the credit side, she generally kept the children from becoming adults-in-miniature, an achievement that few authors reach. On the whole, their conversation seems natural, especially for that created by an author who had included few children in her novels after *Valley of Decision*. But she seems, at times, in handling the children, to reach for the merely clever; for example, the children refer to their nurse, Miss Scope, as "horror-scope," and one child assumes her mother's best friend is "Sally Money" because she has so often heard her speak of alimony. Nevertheless, Mrs. Wharton has a sharp ear for speech, especially when she re-creates the quarrels among the parents. She conveys consummately, for example, the boredom of Joyce Wheater, Judith's mother, when she murmurs to her cigarette, "It's impossible to make Cliffe feel nuances" (53). Her beauty, in fact, provides her only consolation: "She considered her shining nails, as if glassing her indolent beauty in them" (151).

Perhaps Mrs. Wharton's failure to develop the relationship between Judith Wheater and the mature Rose Sellars is disappointing. If she had had more patience with her subject, she might have developed it with the power and the insight that were at her command in *The Reef*, in which she explored so firmly the conflict between Sophy Viner and the mature Anna Leath. Her failure in *The Children* to exhaust the psychic potential of this situation, indeed, prevents this novel from being more than a good one. We must grant that a novel of manners has stylized patterns which interfere with the full development of the characters, but Edith Wharton could have penetrated more deeply and more subtly into the central situation than she does.

The externalized approach does provide some esthetic compensations, however. The farcical nature of the principal scenes and the comic flavor with which Edith Wharton conceives her central characters, including Martin Boyne, provide a stark contrast not only to the poignant situations involving the children but also to the disappointments and painful bewilderment of the middle-aged lovers. Interspersed among the scenes of comic-fantasy are the more somber and realistically envisioned situations involving the more fully developed characters who still retain, as we have seen, some aura of the comic about them.

Such rapid shifting from reality to artifice in the total conspectus of *The Children* and *Twilight Sleep* led some readers to conclude that Edith Wharton had, in her full maturity, lost touch with the realities of modern life. These novels prove, rather, that she had kept abreast of the times and could judge some of the more blatant aspects of the post-war age for the shams that they were. Her critics sometimes failed to see the caustic truth underlying her characters' heightened dialogue and her farcical distortions of character and situation. Both novels reveal that she retained intact a remarkable creative energy and a comic zest which allowed her to assimilate into satiric fiction a new and abrasive culture to which she was, in some respects, fundamentally antagonistic.

CHAPTER 9

Hudson River Bracketed *and*
The Gods Arrive

I *The Development of the Artist as a Passionate Man*

A LTHOUGH Edith Wharton did not visit America in the last
fifteen years of her life, she recognized in *Hudson River
Bracketed* (1929) and in *The Gods Arrive* (1932) the changes
wrought by the Great Depression in the everyday living of
Americans. Despite the tendency of critics to disregard these novels,
they are books of magnitude, interest, and merit. Although they are
not among her greatest works, they attain a respectable position in
her canon and are novels that round out with distinction a literary
career of some forty years. Intellectually, they represent a culmination of many of Edith Wharton's earlier preoccupations; for she
dramatizes in these novels the struggle of the artist to find his own
voice, his need to establish a meeting-ground between the demands
of his integrity and of the marketplace, the relationship of his voca-
tion to his life as a person, the positive effects upon him of feminine
interest in his work, and the destructive effects upon him of irresponsible passion. These two novels are in part the outcome of Edith
Wharton's extensive but often postponed plans for the never-
completed novel, *Literature*, which was begun in 1915 and which
was to have traced the development of a writer. These two novels
also provide a significant reflection of her views on trends in
literature during her later years and are therefore essential to a full
understanding of her esthetic views and practice.

The novels chronicle Vance Weston's emergence as a writer from
his first short story to his successful novels, but they also chronicle
the closely related subject of his love life. His first relationship ends
in disillusionment with the promiscuous Floss Delaney in Euphoria,
Illinois; and this affair is succeeded by a disturbing marriage to
lovely and dependent Laura Lou Tracy who dies at the end of the
first book. Thereafter, and at the heart of both novels, is his life with

Halo Tarrant, who inspires him as a platonic influence in the first book and who becomes his mistress in the second. Throughout the two novels, Mrs. Wharton focuses intensively upon Vance Weston's achievement of identity as a writer and of his growing awareness as a man.

After Vance's abortive relationship with Floss, he leaves the Midwest to live with his distant relatives, the Tracys, in rural New York. He is relatively innocent and has hoped to become a writer by absorbing the sophisticated life of New York City. To his dismay, he is disappointed in all such expectations when he finds himself in a run-down house in a rural area at some distance from the city, an area which, if anything, is more isolated and backward than his home town. His impoverished relatives clean and care for "The Willows," which was described in an 1842 book on architecture as the best example of Hudson River Bracketed, an ornate mode characterized by irregular narrow balconies supported with wooden brackets. But "The Willows" is crucial to Vance's career, though he does not realize it at the time. In the tiny library at "The Willows," he discovers the "Past" and becomes convinced that, through familiarity with the literary tradition which he can gain by perusing the old books there, he will become, like Samuel Taylor Coleridge, a distinguished writer. Halo Spear, a relative of the Tracys, who is a few years older than Vance, eagerly volunteers to be his intellectual guide as he plans to immerse himself in the classics.

Intellectual ambition does not represent for Vance his only fulfillment at the time. His emotional nature demands recognition; and as a result, he persuades the gentle, naive Laura Lou Tracy to break her engagement to the enterprising Bunny Hayes and to elope with him. But their relationship, far from harmonious, is tragic for Laura Lou. Because Vance has to discipline himself in order to write, he ignores her loneliness. A complication supervenes also when Vance retreats to "The Willows" in search of a more relaxing atmosphere for writing each day. Halo begins regularly to meet him to help him with his novel.

Local gossips, particulary Mrs. Tracy, interpret these meetings to Laura Lou as sexual infidelity. Dissension between husband and wife reaches new intensity when Vance takes Laura Lou to the city after his first success. While he makes the rounds of social and literary New York and becomes involved in maneuvering for an important prize, Laura Lou lives a lonely existence in a boarding house. All is not to be smooth for Vance in the city either. Halo Spear's husband, a magazine editor, Lewis Tarrant, hires Vance, exploits him financially, and eventually fires him. Though Vance's first novel sells phenomenally, he receives little money from it.

Toward the end of *Hudson River Bracketed*, Vance and Laura Lou find an abandoned house at the edge of the city and live there in extreme poverty for months. So as not to disturb Vance's frustrating work on another novel, Laura Lou heroically hides the fact that she is hemorrhaging from tuberculosis. In the closing scene of *Hudson River Bracketed*, Halo Spear finds the Westons after much searching, announces to Vance that she has separated from Tarrant, and learns a moment later that Laura Lou has just died. Halo's arrival anticipates the second book, in which Edith Wharton details Halo's life with Vance, particularly as it relates to their troubled personal relationship and to her attempts to shape his work.

Blake Nevius declares that none of the many artists in Edith Wharton's work bears the stamp of authenticity.[1] He overstates the case, however, although Vance's personal problems are often more important and interesting than Mrs. Wharton's presentation of his career as artist. The books center more around the women he loves, his social position, and his constant fight to get money for survival than they do around the mastery of his craft. However, he does provide a voice through which Edith Wharton can express her views, and his activities and struggles as a writer are grim enough. In fact, Mrs. Wharton's involvement with Vance makes him, in some respects, the most believable and interesting artist in her fiction. Granted that she satirized Vance's romanticism as he finds himself inspired by "that celestial Beauty which haunted earth and sky and the deeps of his soul" and that she tended at such times to forget his mundane responsibilities, he emerges as her more authentic spokesman because he is not idealized.

Through Vance, Mrs. Wharton reiterates some principles about literature she held throughout her career, such as the artist's obligation to select detail and his need to reveal a structural sense in his work. In the two books she also voices through him or through his mentor, Halo Spear, her views on the literature of the 1920's and 1930's. When either Vance or Halo expresses sensible views on the nature of literature, a loquacious writer or editor advances opposing ideas. The result is a further exposition of some of Vance's or Halo's principles in the form of a literary dialogue with spirited antagonists. Vance and Halo denounce the superficiality of young writers who are commercially ambitious, the pessimism of Naturalist authors, and the fragmentation of personality which Edith Wharton felt was induced in a character by the use of the stream-of-consciousness technique. Vance certainly speaks for her whenever he discusses writing, especially when he tries to analyze his problems as a writer of fiction. In her description through Vance of the creative process, Edith Wharton resembles Henry James with his idea of the donnée from which all else is derived. The imagination builds upon a single fragment of fact — a single kernel which the author separates from all others and plants in his mind to grow independently. The artist must learn to observe economy both in his personal life and in his art, for they depend on each other. This principle of moderation in all things Vance learns as he leaves "The Willows" after his first visit at the beginning of *Hudson River Bracketed*. Edith Wharton relates this principle to the action at several points in *The Gods Arrive* since Halo's failure to understand it precipitates the rift between her and Vance and causes some of Vance's problems and misfortunes. Too much intense experience upsets Vance; his abnormally keen sensibility can only accommodate a certain amount of stimulation if he is to do his best work: "When the impressions were too abundant and powerful, they benumbed him" *(Gods,* 37).[2] In Spain, for instance, Vance grows lazy; and he seems to have lost even his desire to store his sensations for use in his future work, precisely because they are too abundant here for him to value correctly. We suspect that Edith Wharton suffered from a similar surfeit of experience during the World War I period when she postponed indefinitely the actual composition of *Literature* and other novels and when she could not write *A Son at the Front* until she was further removed in time from her war experience.

When Vance visits Chartres, he suspects that he may have already heard too much about its alleged sublimity. He is not surprised that his reactions to it are dulled, but he is bitterly disappointed that he has lost his capacity to respond to a monument that he recognizes with his intellect to be a great work of art. He is later reassured when he is able to react spontaneously to the simpler beauty of a small church in which he seeks refuge during a storm. In the lightning flashes he glimpses a "fragment of heaven" and sits "among these bursts of glory and passages of darkness as if alternate cantos of the *Paradiso* and the *Inferno* were whirling through him" *(Gods,* 80). Just as the childhood memory of the River Dudden inspired the adult William Wordsworth, so the mere sights and sounds of a river can become for Vance the small, secreted treasures that feed creativity.

Edith Wharton frequently refers, through Vance's voice, to the problems a young writer encounters in trying to maintain his originality and independence. Critics, editors, the influence of other writers, and even the reading of books are all suspect. Vance distrusts critics because, as Halo remarks, they change their standards every day. Halo and, somewhat later, Vance suspect the disinterestedness of editors since they must apply, in the main, commercial criteria to their judgment of art. Editors discourage Vance from being original and prefer him to write in the future what sold well in the past: "the principle of the quick turnover applied to brains as it was to real estate." In her own essays, Edith Wharton found troubling the fact that some of her younger contemporaries refused to read great literature lest they endanger their originality and become derivative in their art. Halo, like Edith Wharton, saw immersion in the tradition as essential to a writer; and she magisterially comments about the New York literary set that "the clever young writers . . . had read only each other and *Ulysses*" (*Gods*, 46).

As a young writer, Vance faces frustration because he can easily copy the facile improvisations and stylistic tricks of his contemporaries but longs to communicate his own vision of the world and his sense of the stark forces that determine man's fate. Edith Wharton herself as a younger writer was undoubtedly annoyed by reviewers who spoke of her cleverness and epigrammatic prose when she was trying to probe deeply into human problems. Vance voices the young author's self-doubt about whether a book composed easily can be good and whether a best-seller can have lasting value. Edith Wharton's own work shows little correlation between the time and effort spent on a novel and its financial success. She herself refused to value as her best works those that sold best. But even in the 1920's she felt the same frustration that Vance voices about the difficulty of his evaluating his own work in the light of hostile criticism.

Again like Edith Wharton in her critical works, Vance distrusts the stream-of-consciousness technique, popular among the other young writers in Paris and in New York. In *The Gods Arrive*, his friends contend that "the art of narrative and the portrayal of social groups had reached its climax" and that now the only hope for attaining new dimensions in fiction is in "the exploration of the subliminal" (*Gods*, 112). But Edith Wharton, to the end, saw the use of a structured plot and of dialogue as more effective methods of characterization than the random probing of the inner psyche; and she rebelled against the formlessness, as she saw it, of the stream-of-consciousness technique.

To Vance — as it probably did to Edith Wharton — the stream-of-consciousness technique inevitably associated itself with a deterministic pessimism, derived in large part from the literary Naturalists, though originally these Naturalists had not made much use of the detailed examination of the inner psyche or done much with experimentation in form. While Mrs. Wharton's own work as early as *The House of Mirth* showed the influence of Naturalism, she never fully subscribed to its deterministic tenets; and stream-of-consciousness fiction tends, in Vance's words, to reduce characters "to bundles of loosely tied instincts and habits, borne along blindly on the current of existence" *(Gods,* 112), and inevitably, therefore, to minimize their power of free choice. Like Vance's most sensitive contemporaries, he wants to depict a reality as it is, no matter how somber; but he wants to see a whole man "pitted against a hostile universe and surviving, and binding it to his own uses" *(Gods,* 113).

Edith Wharton also felt that Naturalist novelists tended to use either sensational or grotesque characters to the point of their soon becoming stereotypes. She expressed her dissatisfaction with this tendency in many of her contemporaries through a young Englishman, Chris Churley, and his comments about current American writing. He derides the two extremes in popular fiction, Romantic historical novels and documentary Naturalist novels, since both evince undeveloped characters. He does not understand, furthermore, why modern writers disregard in their work the middle class which comprises so much that is essentially American; instead, these authors choose to write about princesses in Tuscan villas or ignorant peasants, "gaunt young men with a ten-word vocabulary who spend their lives sweating and hauling wood . . . . There's really nothing as limited as the primitive passions — except perhaps those of princesses" (*Gods,* 176).

II *The Satire of the Superficial and the Provincial*

Beyond her views on literature, Edith Wharton expressed through Vance her scorn for time-serving authors and the venality that motivates them. Her satire may be excessive in depicting the young writers and artists at the Loafers Club and the Coconut Tree Restaurant in New York or at Lorry Spear's apartment in Paris. They are at least dedicated to what they are doing despite their superficiality and false sophistication. But her ridicule of current modes of writing fiction is inescapable and amusing, if sometimes a bit too broad and farcical. The tendencies that she condemned perhaps did not deserve all the attention that she awarded them. But, when her young writers discuss popular novels like *Price of Meat*, now in its seventieth thousand, or *Egg Omelette* (the latter's sales boosted by pulpit denunciations of it), they demonstrate how ridiculous any fad in art can become. Likewise, the quarrel of a prize committee over a book's "exact degree of indecency" and the maneuvering by writers and publishers for the Pulsifer Prize are amusing and contemporaneous aspects of *Hudson River Bracketed* and *The Gods Arrive*. They recall the machinations of George Gissing's characters in the literary world of the 1890's in *The New Grub Street*.

The high-powered parties designed to promote the sales of books and to publicize the reputations of writers also come under Mrs. Wharton's steady scrutiny — parties, for example, in which a woman presses an author to identify the originals of his characters and to verify her suspicion that his love scenes reflect his personal life. With the good humor born of long experience with book promotions, she can even laugh indulgently in *Hudson River Bracketed* at the publicity given to books by newspaper interviews with authors: "The heart-to-heart kind . . . . With a snapshot of yourself looking at the first crocus in your garden; or smoking a pipe, with your arm around a Great Dane" (*Hudson*, 171).

While Edith Wharton's satire is often biting and precise, at other times it is maladroit, even crude, less controlled than that in *Twilight Sleep* and in *The Children*. In her depiction of the rich, ostentatious tourists in *The Gods Arrive*, she attacked them too directly and harshly; she seemed oblivious to the possibility that her attack might have been outdated because the United States was in the depths of the Depression when this novel appeared and most of the wealthy people of the 1920's had become impoverished. Her satire was, for example, out of place in such comments as "If you're going to buy a Rolls-Royce, buy two — it pays in the end" or "We've run down a little place at last where you can really count on the caviar" (*Gods*, 215).

Even more difficult to defend is her snobbish treatment of Vance's Midwestern background and his lack of literary sophistication. For a college graduate interested in the arts, he is impossibly ignorant of literature; American colleges could not have been so provincial as Mrs. Wharton makes them out to be. So his remark to Halo, a stranger, when he skims a book by Coleridge, "Why did no one ever tell me about the Past before?" is totally false (*Hudson*, 50). American education would have done better in those days by Vance than to acquaint him only with James Whitcomb Riley, Ella Wheeler Wilcox, John Greenleaf Whittier, Henry Wadsworth Longfellow, James Russell Lowell, and a little Walt Whitman. Halo Spear is disdainful, as a cultured Easterner, about the Midwest and its purported lack of culture; she imagines that Vance's classmates in the sixth grade were young "savages" about to "maul" the selections in their readers, like "The Ancient Mariner." Though Mrs. Wharton amused readers with her choice of names — like Prune, Nebraska; and Hallelujah, Missouri — her ridicule of the Midwest through her derision of the forces and the milieu that molded her central character misfired. If Vance is an original genius, as Mrs. Wharton would allege, his region must have contributed more to his development than she is willing to admit.

Yet Mrs. Wharton did have some sympathy for small-town life and regarded some aspects of it with indulgent humor. Vance's father, the real-estate promoter (who names his son "Advance" after his land development in Missouri), and Vance's mother and sisters, with their concern for status, are authentic representatives of the American small town in the 1930's. Their bungalow living room reflects Edith Wharton's interest in interiors and is a typical room for a middle-class house in any town in the United States at this time. The gold-and-grey wallpaper, the phonograph on the library table, the crocheted tablecloth, the religious pictures in Woolworth frames, and the houseplant on a milking stool were ubiquitous "props" in 1930. Realistic, too, and humorous is the general evasiveness characterizing the funeral when quotations from Isaiah and James Whitcomb Riley are "intermingled with a practiced hand" and the word "died" is replaced by "passed over."

Edith Wharton's presentation of provincial life is to be measured largely in terms of the skill with which she envisions her minor characters, Grandpa and Grandma Scrimser, for example. Grandma's ranging and mercurial evangelism is suddenly in demand for lectures in the living rooms of wealthy women in New York. She is an older and more solid version of Pauline Manford in *Twilight Sleep* and of Julia Brant in *A Son at the Front.* An elderly "new woman," Grandma scandalizes her children and grandchildren by her uninhibited behavior. This time the children of a wayward parent are scandalized, not the parents of wayward children. As an evangelist, Grandma is an interesting variation on the religious charlatan in Edith Wharton's other fiction and in a novel like Sinclair Lewis' *Elmer Gantry.* She is more sincere than the evangelists who are typically satirized and feels that she gives something of value to the people whose money she takes. She does, however, confide to Vance that baking gingerbread to sell to the neighbors in Missouri was harder work than "coaxing folks back to Jesus."

Grandpa Scrimser, more unscrupulous, is a variation of the small-town elderly lecher. As a youth, Vance experiences much revulsion when he discovers that Floss Delaney is Scrimser's mistress as well as his own. But Vance comes to pity as well as hate Grandpa when a stroke fells the old man and Vance takes him home from the hotel bar; he is a pitiable figure, "like a marionette with its wires cut, propped on the sofa to which they had hurriedly raised him" (*Hudson*, 146). Ironically, when Vance returns to Euphoria as a successful author, he visits with Floss Delaney in the remodelled bar of the hotel (which she now owns) and realizes that Floss seems to have forgotten Grandpa's very existence.

Although Edith Wharton lacked in these two books some of the perceptiveness and practical detachment that had characterized her satire in her earlier works, she revealed, nevertheless, a remarkable capacity to document a social group, to create minor characters in a quick phrase or two, and to evoke a milieu entirely appropriate to the individuals and the events which dominate the novels.

III *Halo Spear: The Dilemma of the "New Woman"*

In *The Gods Arrive*, Edith Wharton concentrated upon the relationship between Halo Tarrant and Vance Weston which had begun early in *Hudson River Bracketed* before Vance's marriage to Laura Lou. The relationship, as Edith Wharton portrays it, lacks some dimension of veracity, though it is full of interest in many ways. There are some inconsistencies and weaknesses in Vance's characterization. Mrs. Wharton does less well with Halo Spear and seems unable to attain a viable balance between the opposing forces in Halo; and, as a result, Halo emerges as a less sympathetic individual than the author intended her to be. Mrs. Wharton is perhaps not critical enough of Halo's unscrupulousness, her materialism, her egotism, and her selfishness. Halo hardly represents the graciousness of tradition when she argues that her family would have difficulty conversing at dinner if they were to invite their poor relatives, the Tracys, along with Vance: "They talk another language. It can't be helped" (*Hudson*, 87). Condescension and a certain envy mark her attitude toward Vance's creative work from the moment when she interrupts his reading at "The Willows" on his first visit, yet Edith Wharton also inconsistently regarded her as one whose real gift "was for appreciating the gifts of others" (*Hudson*, 84). Other aspects of her actions and motivations seem to be contradictions which Mrs. Wharton does not reconcile, rather than complexities that add richness to Halo's character.

Fortunately, Halo Spear in *The Gods Arrive* is not the same woman in *Hudson River Bracketed*; and this change may be partly, but not entirely, explained by her having attained greater experience and maturity. In the earlier book, she showed a servile willingness to marry Lewis Tarrant for his money and prestige and for the opportunity marriage gave her to leave Paul's Landing for New York City. Edith Wharton tended to equate Halo's limited economic opportunities with those that had been open to Lily Bart in *The House of Mirth* at the turn of the century: "Even had discipline and industry fostered her slender talents, they would hardly have brought her a living . . . what else was there for her but marriage?" (*Hudson*, 84). The total lack of confidence in Halo's ability to earn her own living is inconsistent with the impression that Halo elsewhere conveys of being a character who has enough confidence in herself to bolster Vance's faltering ego in his struggles to realize himself as a writer.

In *The Gods Arrive*, Halo is nothing if not independent; a "new woman," she prefers not to marry Vance, even after Tarrant reluctantly grants her a divorce. Together she and Vance tour Europe for the sake of providing him with inspiration and subject matter for his books. Though society insults and excludes her, Halo refuses to impose sexual and social restrictions upon her lover; and Edith Wharton's own ambivalent feelings about the value of marriage probably appear here. When Halo declares that she wants Vance to feel as free as air, she is reminded paradoxically that a woman who refuses to marry may be chaining her lover all the tighter: "The defenseless woman, and all that. If you were his wife, you and he'd be on a level" (*Gods*, 313). The situation in which a woman idealizes her role of mistress when a man advocates marriage had appeared early and frequently in Mrs. Wharton's short stories and had already arisen in the 1920's in both *A Son at the Front* and in *Twilight Sleep*. In *The Gods Arrive*, Mrs. Wharton might have been commenting subtly on the fact that American men were thought to be more chivalrous to the unmarried women they loved than to their wives.

Halo's experiences as Vance's mistress are both inspiriting and distressing. She defends herself vigorously against the criticism of her

brother Lorry who hypocritically resents her visiting him, although
he lives with a mistress as do his bohemian friends in Paris:
"Naturally a man feels differently about his sister." With some conviction, Mrs. Wharton presents marriage, not as a more virtuous
alternative to free love, but as a stabilizing institution that prevents a
person's life from becoming unduly chaotic. Marriage keeps life in
balance as Frenside, the wise philosopher, declares: "We most of us
need a frame-work, a support — the maddest lovers do. Marriage
may be too tight a fit — may dislocate and deform. But it shapes life
too; prevents lopsidedness or drifting" (Gods, 311). Marriage also
becomes a kind of insurance against the inevitable breaking up of
strong love — the cynical, but humane, answer to the sometimes
ephemeral nature of sexual love. Marriage, by retaining the mere
forms of love, prevents the violent tearing up of dying roots, which
may still on occasion be reinvigorated. Vance finally sees marriage as
providing a way for two people who had once filled each other's universe to hold together as the tide of natural passion and intense involvement recedes.

Actually, Halo's intellectual superiority — sometimes presented as
genuine, at other times, as specious — is what Vance comes to re-
sent. The love affair runs aground when Vance resents Halo's
dominating influence on his writing and his intellectual growth. The
appearance of his old flame, Floss Delaney, for whom surprisingly he
feels some of his former passion revive, threatens further complications.

Halo's relationship to Vance provides the major focus of the novel,
however, a relationship characterized by much poignancy despite
Halo's occasional limitations as a person. For her, sex indissolubly
merges with her interest in Vance as an artist; and she can hardly
think of love in any terms other than intellectual. She buries her own
ambition in order to support her lover's, only to find that she has
transferred her own intense ambition to her lover who becomes increasingly restive under the pressure that she exerts. To Halo, the
man must succeed in order to satisfy the woman who stands behind
him and finds her aspirations satisfied vicariously by his success. The
compulsion upon the man in such a case may become unbearable as
it does with Vance.

Vance's frustrated love and his desertion of Halo arise from his
resentment of the intellectual and artistic pressures that she thrusts
upon him, although her interest in his writing had fostered their
early love and contributed signally to his own success. He had

responded sexually to her in *Hudson River Bracketed* when he first sensed that her imagination was flowing through his and inflaming him as he planned his first novel. In *The Gods Arrive*, she has had to become more passive in her influence: "she listened intelligently, but she no longer collaborated" (*Gods*, 72). To this extent, her love as she envisioned it has diminished; she is no longer apparently the chief source of her lover's inspiration; and he may, in fact, have developed beyond her powers to bring him out further. She can never fully accept his view, expressed several months later, of the artist's dependence upon the criticism of others: "My dear child — shall I give you the cold truth . . . the artist asks other people's opinions to please *them* and not to help himself" (*Gods*, 337).

Because Halo insists on loving the artist as well as the man, her love becomes finally a repressive influence upon the man she is ironically straining to serve. For him, she becomes "a reproach and a torment," when all he wants is to collect his own thoughts in contemplative peace: "The absorbing interest of seeing his gift unfold under her care had been so interwoven with her love that she could not separate them" (*Gods*, 28). A kind of masochism underlies her wish to be subservient to his talent as she asks herself, " 'Shall I have to content myself with being a peg to hang a book on?' and found an anxious joy in the idea" (*Gods*, 36). Vance resents her expectant watching for his reactions to new experience, her monitoring of his progress as a potential artist. At Chartres, he grows sulky and baffled and declares he cannot see what she expects him to see. It is as if he has failed her sexual demands and become suddenly impotent before a curious and excessively sympathetic woman: "Halo was elaborately tactful; she waited, she kept silent; she left him to his emotions; but no emotions came . . . . The masculine longing to be left alone was uppermost; he wanted to hate Chartres without having to give any reason" (*Gods*, 78 - 9).

Halo's emasculating care of Vance extends to his manuscripts themselves. The result is that his frustrations — and her suffering from his rejection — intensify. His books for her become phallic emblems when she judges each new work in terms of its relationship to his masculinity. She resents any lesser book of his as a kind of sexual affront to her, as though it were a symbol of personal weakness and depleted vigor on Vance's part and an insult to her own protective femininity: "What business had a man of Weston's quality to be doing novels like ladies' fancy-work . . . . The next book . . . will show them all what he really is . . . . There were times when she caught herself praying for that next book as lonely wives pray for a child" (*Gods*, 85 - 6). Later, when she fears that he may be merely following literary fashion in his new novel, instead of expressing his individuality as she knows it, she resents his hiding the manuscript from her; and she equates such furtiveness with a husband's hiding the evidence of sexual infidelity. She refuses to look at the manuscript, just as she would refuse to spy on an affair: "If there had been a letter from a woman in that drawer, she reflected, it would have been almost easier to resist looking at it" (*Gods*, 100).

Edith Wharton handled with sympathy and insight Vance's desertion of Halo and her sufferings from this separation in the last chapters of *The Gods Arrive*. Halo simply returns to "The Willows" where her supreme adventure with Vance had begun and mechanically devotes herself to gardening. She refuses to think or feel, and she only responds to the heat of the sun on her neck and the fatigue in her muscles. She tries to kill her suffering by not allowing it to surface to her conscious mind and by resolutely turning her energies to physical pursuits.

Halo's final recognition that Vance had resented her part in his work is more bitter to her than the waning of his passion. Cynically, she had acknowledged that passion cannot last, but she had had faith that a deeper understanding underlay their particular love. "The intellectual divorce" between them became more bitter to her than their physical separation. Conversely, the fact that Halo has allowed this intellectual divorce to occur frees Vance for a renewal of his passion for Halo in the last scene in which he discovers she is pregnant and approaches her simply as a child approaches a protective maternal figure. He wishes her to protect him and to be, in a sense, a mother to him as well as to the child that they have conceived. Vance is not yet ready to accept the intellectual companionship of a woman, though, as a sensitive man, he may eventually be able to do so. In the last scene, he sees her as at one with the soil and the sun in her garden. She is back in "the Past" at "The Willows," and she is at one with nature in her pregnancy. She has, in these respects, fulfilled the romantic dreams that Vance previously associated with her. Perhaps the sincerity that imbues his romanticism will also develop in the future into a full appreciation of Halo's distinction, for Halo has been refined and matured by the suffering which she has in part brought on herself.

CHAPTER 10

The Buccaneers *and*
Another Backward Glance

I The Buccaneers: *An Old Theme, a New Hope*

I N *The Buccaneers* (1938), Edith Wharton returned to the theme she had developed in many shorter works and in her three greatest novels: *The House of Mirth, The Custom of the Country,* and *The Age of Innocence* — the comparative value of modernity and tradition. Like *The Age of Innocence, The Buccaneers* takes place in the 1870's; but more in this than in any of her earlier novels, Mrs. Wharton emphasizes the positive qualities in young Americans, the conscientiousness and the seriousness in the children of the rising middle class, and a more satiric approach to European nobility. Reflecting the milieu of the 1930's as well as of the 1870's, she reveals her own concern for the welfare of workers and their families in her treatment of a disagreement between the young Duke and Duchess of Tintagel.

The buccaneers are five young American women — Lizzie and Mab Elmsworth, Virginia and Annabel (Nan) St. George, and Conchita Closson. They enliven a Saratoga summer resort, while their ambitious mothers sit on the porches of the lodge, fanning themselves, eyeing other guests critically, and wondering what the menu in the hotel dining room will be. No less ambitious socially, but wanting more excitement, their fathers closely watch for glamorous women guests and new business prospects.

The individualism and the eagerness for change that characterize the buccaneers promise an invigorating and freshening force in European as well as in American society. Disappointed the next winter in their attempts to crash New York society, the energetic buccaneers decide to conquer London and marry into nobility. Their high spirits, their defiance of stodgy conventions, and their determination to win what they want lend their enterprise a vitality and a

137

confidence that contrast with the complacency of the conservative older generation in both America and England. Miss Laura Test-valley, the thirty-nine-year-old Italian governess of Nan St. George, directs the campaign; and she also provides the indispensable link between the two generations. While the tone of the novel usually is light and ingratiating, Mrs. Wharton's insistent irony modulates the comedy since the men and the society which the buccaneers conquer are, after all, not really worthy of their beauty, intelligence, and courageous spirits.

Mrs. Wharton spent her last four or five years writing the fragment, and it was edited by Gaillard Lapsley and published the year after her death, with her plot outline and a long essay, "A Note on The Buccaneers," by Lapsley. By the end of the fragment, one of the women has married a civil servant, and the others have married British noblemen. Most importantly, Nan St. George has been for some time the Duchess of Tintagel; has suffered a miscarriage; has just fallen in love with a baronet, Guy Thwarte; and has announced her intention to divorce the Duke of Tintagel. The synopsis indicates that Mrs. Wharton intended that Nan would leave her husband, the duke and elope with the baronet, Guy Thwarte, and that Laura Test-valley would sacrifice her own chances for a good marriage with Sir Helmsley Thwarte by assisting in this elopement of his son and a divorced woman. The fragment deviates from the author's synopsis in that the Elmsworth girls figure less importantly in the novel than they did in the plan; Miss Testvalley, who had seemed destined to be the protagonist in the synopsis, becomes relatively minor in her function in the plot, although she is a fascinating personality; and Nan St. George becomes the chief character.

Gaillard Lapsley expressed misgivings about publishing the un-finished work of an author so given to extensive revision, but he decided that the several existing sections should not be withheld and that publication would give readers an insight into the work of a careful craftsman at a midpoint in the creation of an important work.[1] Louis Auchincloss dismisses *The Buccaneers* as a novel just as well left unfinished.[2] On the other hand, Geoffrey Walton has more recently viewed the book as the work that would have been most significant in the last twenty years of Mrs. Wharton's career had she completed it.[3] He thinks it would have equalled her early master-pieces, and he sees in it a new revelation of her need to achieve a social reintegration by balancing the traditions and dignity of the

Old World with the sincerity and energy of the New. To him, Edith Wharton's vision of an emerging harmony between the classes would have possessed intellectual weight and emotional richness.

Much of what can be said about an uncompleted work must be conjecture based upon an assumption of what the finished work would have become, but the probability is that Edith Wharton might have made this novel her most interesting one since *The Age of Innocence*. Certainly Nan Tintagel and Laura Testvalley would have been strong characters; and Ushant, the Duke of Tintagel, even in the present sketch of him, is one of her finest minor characters. Mrs. Wharton in the early part of the book takes a slightly amused view of her characters and their social ambitions. A good-natured tone underlies her descriptions, for instance, of Mrs. St. George sipping her lemonade on the verandah of the Saratoga hotel while she looks forward to entering the dining room with her husband because he is the most handsome man in the hotel. But her excessive pride in him makes her vulnerable to fears that all the women in the resort are conspiring to win him from her, especially some whom she vaguely identifies as "the dreadful painted women . . . who leered and beckoned . . . under the fringes of their sunshades" and other more fashionable ladies whom she characterizes as ones who wear pink bonnets. Mrs. St. George herself would like to be more stylish, but she longs for the good old days when fashion flattered the slightly plump — with crinoline petticoats and dresses "looped up at the hem like drawing-room draperies." The broomlike silhouette now in style, with all the material gathered at the hips, she sees as another conspiracy against her. If Mrs. Wharton treats Mrs. St. George with some ridicule, she is compassionate in understanding her fears and her isolation when she must leave her husband to accompany the buccaneers on their European campaign.

The Europeans, as well as the Americans, are the subject of the same friendly satire, though it at times carries more sting. The Duke of Tintagel, who loves to repair clocks, absent-mindedly forgets his mission, no matter where he is, if he finds a clock not working properly. He holds it to his ear as gently and as thoughtfully as a doctor who is diagnosing a heart condition. Having greatness thrust upon him by inheritance, he longs to be an ordinary citizen who could simply wind his own clocks in peace. The Duke's father, Mrs. Wharton also depicts with kindly ridicule: "The late Duke had had no vices; but his virtues were excessively costly" (165).[4] Among other costs imposed by his accepting too seriously the responsibilities of his dukedom, the old Duke of Tintagel fathered eight daughters in the tedious attempt to produce an heir.

Lord Brightlingsea, who becomes father-in-law to two of the buccaneers, can never remember without his wife's prompting who Miss March is. Yet Miss March is the American whom he jilted at the church door some twenty-five years before and who has devotedly remained in England for the pleasure of watching his family grow up.

The latter half of the fragment successfully exploits the mock-heroic approach. Conchita Closson, already married to Lord Seadown, leaves for England and establishes a military outpost for the campaign soon to be launched by the others. Laura Testvalley, upon landing in England, becomes a scout to survey the territory before battle plans are drawn. She calls upon Miss March and enlists the defeated soldier of the last generation in another battle of American women against English noblemen. Miss March sits in her little London house planning strategy; she is eager to play a secret part in a new adventure, for she feels a kinship with these young "marauders."

The high point of the warfare occurs when Lady Churt descends upon the young women in the garden at Runnymede in a fit of jealousy, and a fiery scene ensues. Lady Churt, who has rented her cottage to the buccaneers, discovers that her lover, Lord Richard, is still a frequent guest at the cottage in her absence because he is attracted to both Lizzie Elmsworth and Virginia St. George. When the invader in her fury seems to be besting the buccaneers and the embarrassed Lord Richard, Lizzie, who has been jealous of Virginia, suddenly joins forces with her against the enemy; and she suggests in an imperious tone that it is the proper moment for Lord Richard and Virginia to announce their engagement. Routed by this strategy, Lady Churt and her straggling troops find their way back to her motorcar.

The novel remains hilarious and farcical in its fast movement. We recognize that the buccaneers gain the field against an enemy more than willing to be conquered — the enemy who are men. However, a more serious tone pervades the scenes near the end in which Nan Tintagel plans to divorce her husband of almost two years because she is in love with Sir Guy Thwarte. With the book as it presently exists, we can find no adequate justification for the divorce. Ushant, the Duke of Tintagel, can be accused only of dullness and ultraconservatism; and Mrs. Wharton has made him a likeable, if inept, character. Certainly in endorsing Nan's elopement, Mrs. Wharton was going beyond the mores of 1870 and also beyond her own views about the situations that justify divorce or desertion. When divorce occurs in the life of a sympathetic character in Mrs. Wharton's fiction, a strong reason exists for it; and her fictional interest in such cases most often centers in the problems resulting from the divorce or the desertion rather than in the situation that generated the marital discord. In this case, the probable marriage of Nan and Guy Thwarte seems symbolic as a kind of union of two societies, American and English, and as a strong new fusion of the forces of tradition and change. Both parties to the new marriage have pursued at the same time the materialistic and the esthetic without experiencing any sense of futility or of conflict.

As to the British aristocracy, Mrs. Wharton is not without sympathy for it, in spite of her awareness of its occasional moral weaknesses and opportunism. She shows respect for the English nobility in its interest in family stability, in its efficient management of households, in its maintenance of beautiful and historic houses, and in its sense of responsibility to the surrounding community. Nevertheless, she is also aware of the absurdities involved when an impoverished nobleman resorts to all kinds of hypocritical expediency in order to maintain the family estate and when the same nobleman rationalizes his ignoring the general needs of a community by bestowing token attention on the laborers on his estates. While Geoffrey Walton sees "fantastic ignorance, frequent absurdity, and breath-taking hypocrisy" in the British aristocrats in this novel,[5] we also find these same (or similar) characteristics in the newly rich parents of the buccaneers who are invading the British strongholds. The hope set forth in the book would seem to lie less in the influence of Americans on the English than in that of a new kind of young people in both nations who value tradition and art at the same time that they seek change in social patterns.

The direction of the book indicates the error of those who suggest that Edith Wharton's skill in the writing of fiction left her before her death and that, in the latter part of her life, she longed only for the settled past, viewed the present with dissatisfaction, and thought of the future with foreboding. In her seventies, she was a writer whose technical expertise was still developing and whose fictional resources had by no means been depleted.

142

II *A Backward Glance at the Career of Edith Wharton*

In her major works Edith Wharton was able to evoke the
metaphysical and symbolical implications of the situations which she
was presenting. She knew how to maintain the single point of view
while juxtaposing the narrator's varying depths of consciousness in
order to achieve intense dramatic effects. She was also able to give
moments of significant experience permanent form as viable works
of art. She was adept at suggesting dimensions of experience that
would ordinarily escape a literal transcription of it. As a result, she
furnished the sensitive reader with fragmentary clues enabling him
to divine implicitly her interpretation of her subject.

Few critics would challenge either the general acceptance of *The
House of Mirth, The Custom of the Country,* and *The Age of Innocence* as her best novels or the reputation *Ethan Frome* has enjoyed as her best novella. But other works less well known are almost
as good. *The Reef,* for example, represents an incisive analysis of the
tensions resulting from differences in the American and the European points of view, in the generations presented, and in the
masculine and the feminine approach to life. In many of her short
stories, which are not as well known as they should be, she illustrated
in more concentrated fashion than in the novels the careful technique, the evocative style, and the concern for esthetic order which
characterize her work at its best. In several of them she impressively
balanced a meticulous craftsmanship and imaginative power. Her
novellas other than *Ethan Frome* deserve more attention than
readers have been inclined to give them. *Madame de Treymes*
reveals her skill in the analysis of the Jamesian international theme
and in presenting the manifold relationships of "manners," as they
relate, in her characters, to moral issues. *Summer* reveals her extensive probing of complex psychic and social problems of a pregnant
girl. Mrs. Wharton analyzes in it, with full power and insight, a complicated relationship between a young woman and an older man as
the man veers from cruelty and lust toward sympathy and respect
and as the girl veers from revulsion for him and fear of his sexuality
toward toleration and mild liking.

One preconception which must be challenged has become almost
a commonplace in the criticism of Edith Wharton — the assumption
that her artistic powers declined sharply after 1920 and that her work
written in the 1920's and 1930's is negligible. If such late novels as
The Glimpses of the Moon or *The Mother's Recompense* are inferior, others from this period are interesting and accomplished

works; and, as such, they demand close scrutiny. In *The Children* and in *Twilight Sleep* a vein of comic fantasy and a stylized exaggeration of manners sharpen her satire of the irresponsible rich. *Hudson River Bracketed* and *The Gods Arrive* offer penetrating insights into the development of the artist's consciousness and his relationship to a materialistic society. They also offer insights into the artist's sexual life as it affects his work and into the devoted woman's relationship to him. In all of these last novels, Edith Wharton examines the family as both a civilizing and a dehumanizing influence; and she considers, acutely but dispassionately, the psychic and moral consequences that color the lives of those who rebel against conventional sexual standards. Even in *The Buccaneers*, on which she was working at the time of her death, she showed renewed artistic vigor and a fresh mock-heroic approach to her subject. In addition, many of her finest short stories appeared in these last years.

Edith Wharton was prolific and versatile and wrote essays, criticism, short stories, novellas, and novels of undisputable excellence on many subjects. She was also gifted in modulating her style to fit the multifarious characters, situations, and ideas that she developed in these various genres. Her best work reveals her accomplished artistry, her grasp of social reality, her realization that manners are a key to the outer life of a society and the expression of an inner reality that escapes casual observation, her moral subtlety and incisiveness, and her unwavering insight into human nature.

Edith Wharton, seen in perspective, is a novelist who provides a link between the morally and psychologically oriented works of Hawthorne and James, who preceded her, and the later Realists like Sinclair Lewis or F. Scott Fitzgerald with their tendency toward the sardonic and iconoclastic. Edith Wharton may not have been capable of Hawthorne's moral inclusiveness, infinite perceptiveness, and imaginative reach which, as James said, made him "a habitué of a region of mysteries and subleties" where he took as his province "the whole deep mystery of man's soul and conscience . . . the deeper psychology."[6] She may also have been incapable of James's firm but infinitely subtle probing of the human mind and of his dissecting of the various nuances of behavior, conscious or unconscious, in any given scene.

But, like both Hawthorne and James, Edith Wharton was sensitive to the ambiguities in inner experience, in human behavior, and in many generally accepted ethical and metaphysical formulations. More than they, she, of course, understood the intricacies involved in living as a woman in a world set up for the social, economic, and sexual advantage of men. Sensitive as she was to the complications inherent in human motives and values, she tended in her work, as James did in his, to illuminate rather than resolve the complex issues and situations that she subjected to her scrutiny. She drew few simple conclusions about class, society, or individuals. More than James, she had the ability to assimilate natural landscape and urban milieu into her art and to make consummate use of such settings as active factors in the unfolding psychic drama in her work. In this respect she seems closer to Hawthorne than to James.

Critics have generally emphasized her involvement with a dying aristocracy, her skill as a writer of comedies of manners, and her treatment of the interaction between Americans and Europeans. She does manifest these preoccupations, but she is a moralist as well as a mannerist. She transcends the realistic aspects of her world by striking intuitions into the psychic motivations of her characters. Though she did not herself use some of the later techniques of dream, association, distortion, and imagery that enable a writer to penetrate the innermost recesses of a character's psyche, she was, essentially and at her best, a psychologist in fiction. She continued the Jamesian propensity for disengaging "crucial moments from the welter of existence" to ascertain their true worth and significance and to determine how they affect the psyches and moral life of her characters.

Mrs. Wharton augmented nineteenth-century Realism by her intense satirical scrutiny of her materials; and, in this manner, she prepared the way for the satiric Realists of the 1920's such as Sinclair Lewis and Sherwood Anderson. We can hardly doubt that Elmer Moffatt in *The Custom of the Country* was a prototype for *Babbitt* and that Lewis had good cause to dedicate *Babbitt* to her. Her small-town, middle-class people in *Summer* or in *Hudson River Bracketed* are one in spirit with those in Lewis's *Main Street*. The crude and vulgar power of some of Edith Wharton's figures is absent from the more decorous characters of James or Hawthorne.

One of the most reasonable critical judgments passed on Edith Wharton is Q. D. Leavis's 1938 statement: "She was a remarkable novelist if not a large-sized one, and while there are few great novelists, there are not even so many remarkable ones that we can afford to let her be overlooked."[7] In this statement lies the truth currently accepted about Edith Wharton and her importance in the American culture. She was, indeed, a remarkable novelist. She may some day be recognized as a great one.

Notes and References

Chapter One

1. Page numbers in parentheses in this chapter, unless otherwise specified, refer to *A Backward Glance* (New York, 1934).
2. R. W. B. Lewis, *Edith Wharton* (New York, 1975). All information on the affair with Fullerton is based on Lewis's biography, pp. 183 - 232 and 255 - 64, *passim*.
3. Wayne Andrews, "Introduction," *The Best Short Stories of Edith Wharton* (New York, 1958), p. xxi. See also Louis Auchincloss, *Edith Wharton* (St. Paul, 1961), pp. 15 - 16, and Grace Kellogg, *The Two Lives of Edith Wharton* (New York, 1965), p. 119.
4. Agnes Repplier, *American Catholic World* (June, 1902), p. 422; reviews in *Louisville Courier-Journal* and *Boston Evening Transcript;* Charles Eliot Norton in Millicent Bell, *Edith Wharton and Henry James* (New York, 1965), p. 86; Van Wyck Brooks, *The Confident Years* (New York, 1952), p. 287.
5. Percy Lubbock, *The Letters of Henry James* (New York, 1920), I, p. 396.
6. Leon Edel, *Henry James, The Master* (Philadelphia, 1972), p. 251; hereafter referred to in my text as Edel.
7. Helpful in such a comparison is R. P. Blackmur's introduction to Henry James' *The Art of the Novel* (New York, 1934), pp. vii - xxxix. He discusses in detail the themes and techniques that James considers in his prefaces and illustrates in his fiction.
8. R. W. B. Lewis, *Edith Wharton*, p. 382.
9. Grace Kellogg, *The Two Lives of Edith Wharton* (New York, 1965), pp. 209 - 11.
10. To Walter Maynard, in Louis Auchincloss, *Edith Wharton, A Woman in Our Time* (New York, 1971), p. 123.

Chapter Two

1. Unless otherwise specified, page numbers in parentheses in this chapter refer to *The House of Mirth* (New York, 1905).
2. Walter Rideout, "Edith Wharton's *The House of Mirth*," in Charles Shapiro, *Twelve Original Essays* (Detroit, 1958), p. 173; Geoffrey Walton, *Edith Wharton* (Teaneck, 1970), p. 59.
3. Blake Nevius, *Edith Wharton* (Berkeley, 1961), p. 59.

Chapter Three

1. Page numbers in parentheses in this section refer to *The Fruit of the Tree* (New York, 1907).
2. Page numbers in parentheses in this section refer to *The Reef* (New York, 1912).

Chapter Four

1. "Introduction," *Ethan Frome*, Modern Students Library Edition (New York: Charles Scribner's Sons, 1922), p. v.
2. Percy Lubbock, *Portrait of Edith Wharton* (London, 1947), pp. 130 - 31, recounts that she passed a neglected, unpainted farmhouse. She later stopped at the meeting house to spend an hour alone trying to imagine what life would be like for people living in that house.
3. John Crowe Ransom, "Characters and Character," *American Review* (Jan., 1936), 271 - 75; Bernard DeVoto, "Introduction," *Ethan Frome* (New York, 1938), p. xviii; Lionel Trilling, "The Morality of Inertia," *Gathering of Fugitives* (Boston, 1956).
4. *Ethan Frome*, Modern Students Library Edition, pp. vi - vii.

Chapter Five

1. Henry James, "The New Novel," *Notes on Novelists* (New York, 1914), pp. 353 - 56.
2. Blake Nevius, *Edith Wharton*, p. 158.
3. Geoffrey Walton, *Edith Wharton*, p. 108.

Chapter Six

1. Date after title refers to appearance in a collection unless Wharton chose not to include the story in a book. The date, then, as in this case, indicates magazine appearance.
2. R. W. B. Lewis, *The Collected Stories of Edith Wharton*, (Boston, 1971), I, xxvi.

Chapter Seven

1. Unless otherwise specified, page numbers in parentheses in this chapter refer to *The Age of Innocence* (New York, 1920).

2. W. J. Stuckey, *The Pulitzer Prize Novels* (Norman, 1966), pp. 39 - 42.

3. Vernon Parrington, "Our Literary Aristocrat," *Pacific Review* (June, 1921), pp. 157 - 60.

4. Blake Nevius, *Edith Wharton*, p. 178.

5. Joseph Warren Beach, *The Twentieth-Century Novel* (New York, 1932), pp. 291 - 303.

6. Viola Hopkins, "The Ordering Style of *The Age of Innocence*," *American Literature*, XXX (Nov., 1958), 345 - 57. In my analysis of Edith Wharton's imagery, I am indebted to Ms. Hopkins' study.

Chapter Eight

1. Anon., "Profile of Edith Wharton," *The Herald Tribune*, European Edition, Nov. 16, 1936.

2. Letter dated June 8, 1925, in F. Scott Fitzgerald, *The Crack-Up*, ed., Edmund Wilson (New York, 1945), p. 309.

3. Percy Lubbock, *Portrait of Edith Wharton* (New York, 1947), p. 200 - 01.

4. "The Great American Novel," *Yale Review*, XVI (1927), 655.

5. *Fighting France* (New York, 1915), p. 204.

6. Frederick P. Hoffman, *The Twenties* (New York, 1955), pp. 47 - 51.

7. Edmund Wilson, "Twilight Sleep," *New Republic*, 51 (1927), 78.

8. *Ibid.*

9. *Twilight Sleep* (New York, 1927), p. 253.

10. *Ibid.*, p. 113.

11. Q. D. Leavis, "Henry James's Heiress: The Importance of Edith Wharton," *Scrutiny* (Dec., 1938), pp. 269 - 70.

12. Unless otherwise specified, numbers in parentheses in the remainder of this section refer to *The Children* (New York, 1928).

Chapter Nine

1. Blake Nevius, *Edith Wharton* (Berkeley, 1953), p. 20.

2. In this section page numbers in parentheses are designated by a word in the title of *Hudson River Bracketed* (New York, 1929) and of *The Gods Arrive* (New York, 1932).

Chapter Ten

1. Gaillard Lapsley, "A Note on *The Buccaneers*," in *The Buccaneers* (New York, 1938), p. 360.

2. Louis Auchincloss, "Edith Wharton and Her New Yorks," *Partisan Review*, XVIII (1951), p. 419.

3. Geoffrey Walton, *Edith Wharton* (Teaneck, 1970), p. 177.

4. Unless otherwise specified, page numbers in parentheses in this section refer to *The Buccaneers* (New York, 1938).

5. Geoffrey Walton, *Edith Wharton*, p. 184.

6. Henry James, "Hawthorne," in Edmund Wilson, *The Shock of Recognition* (New York, 1947), p. 476.

7. Q. D. Leavis, "Henry James's Heiress: The Importance of Edith Wharton," *Scrutiny* (Dec., 1938), p. 276.

Selected Bibliography

PRIMARY SOURCES

Listed in chronological order of first printing

1. Novels

The Valley of Decision. 2 vols. New York: Scribner's, 1902.

The House of Mirth. New York: Scribner's, 1905; New York: Holt, Rinehart and Winston, 1962; New York: Bantam Books, 1962; Boston: Houghton Mifflin, 1963; New York: New American Library, 1964; London: Constable, 1966.

The Fruit of the Tree. New York: Scribner's, 1907.

The Reef. New York: Appleton, 1912; New York: Scribner's, 1965; Contemporary Editions Series, New York: Scribner's, 1970.

The Custom of the Country. New York: Scribner's, 1913; New York: Scribner's, 1956.

The Age of Innocence. New York: Appleton, 1920; New York: New American Library, 1962; London: Constable, 1966; New York: Scribner's, 1968; Contemporary Classics, New York: Scribner's, 1970.

The Glimpses of the Moon. New York: Appleton, 1922.

A Son at the Front. New York: Scribner's, 1923.

The Mother's Recompense. New York: Appleton, 1925.

Twilight Sleep. New York: Appleton, 1927.

The Children. New York: Appleton, 1928.

Hudson River Bracketed. New York: Appleton, 1929; New York: New American Library, 1962.

The Gods Arrive. New York: Appleton, 1932.

The Buccaneers. New York: Appleton-Century, 1938.

2. Novellas

The Touchstone. New York: Scribner's, 1900.
Sanctuary. New York: Scribner's, 1903.
Madame de Treymes. New York: Scribner's, 1907.
Ethan Frome. New York: Scribner's, 1911; Modern Students Library, New
    York: Scribner's, 1922; New York: Scribner's, 1938; New York:
    Scribner's, 1939; *Ethan Frome: The Story with Sources and Commen-
    tary*, ed. Blake Nevius, New York: Scribner's, 1968; School Paperback,
    New York: Scribner's, 1968.
"Bunner Sisters," *Xingu and Other Stories.* New York: Scribner's, 1916.
Summer. New York: Appleton, 1917; Contemporary Classics, New York:
    Scribner's, 1964.
The Marne. New York: Appleton, 1918.
Old New York: False Dawn, The Old Maid, The Spark, New Year's Day. 4
    vols. New York: Appleton, 1924; New York: Scribner's, 1964.
Quinn, Arthur H., ed., *The Edith Wharton Treasury.* New York: Appleton-
    Century-Crofts, 1950. (Includes part of *The Age of Innocence*, *The
    Old Maid*, "Bunner Sisters," *Madame de Treymes*, and 8 short
    stories).
Madame de Treymes and Others: Four Novellas. New York: Scribner's,
    1970. (Includes *The Touchstone*, *Sanctuary*, and "Bunner Sisters").

3. Short Story Collections

The Greater Inclination. New York: Scribner's, 1899.
Crucial Instances. New York: Scribner's, 1901.
The Descent- of Man and Other Stories. New York: Scribner's, 1904.
The Hermit and the Wild Woman and Other Stories. New York: Scribner's,
    1908.
Tales of Men and Ghosts. New York: Scribner's, 1910.
Xingu and Other Stories. New York: Scribner's, 1916.
Here and Beyond. New York: Appleton, 1926.
Certain People. New York: Appleton, 1930.
Human Nature. New York: Appleton, 1933.
The World Over. New York: Appleton-Century, 1936.
Ghosts. New York: Appleton-Century, 1937. Reprinted as *The Ghost Stories
    of Edith Wharton*, New York: Scribner's, 1973.
Andrews, Wayne, ed. with introduction. *The Best Short Stories of Edith
    Wharton.* New York: Scribner's, 1958.
Roman Fever and Other Stories. New York: Scribner's, 1964. (Includes 8
    stories).
Auchincloss, Louis, ed. with introduction. *The Edith Wharton Reader.* New
    York: Scribner's, 1965.

Lewis, R. W. B., ed. with introduction. *The Collected Short Stories of Edith Wharton.* 2 vols. Boston: Houghton Mifflin, 1971.

4. Poetry

Verses. Newport: C. E. Hammett, 1878.
Artemis to Actaeon and Other Verse. New York: Scribner's, 1909.
Twelve Poems. London: The Medici Society, 1926.

5. Miscellaneous Writings

The Decoration of Houses (with Ogden Codman, Jr.). New York: Scribner's, 1897.
The Joy of Living by Hermann Sudermann, trans. by Edith Wharton. New York: Scribner's, 1902.
Italian Villas and Their Gardens. New York: Century, 1904.
Italian Backgrounds. New York: Scribner's, 1905.
A Motor-Flight Through France. New York: Scribner's, 1908.
Fighting France, from Dunkerque to Belfort. New York: Scribner's, 1915.
The Book of the Homeless, ed. Edith Wharton. New York: Scribner's, 1916.
French Ways and Their Meaning. New York: Appleton, 1919.
In Morocco. New York: Scribner's, 1920.
The Writing of Fiction. New York: Scribner's, 1925; New York: Octagon Books, 1966.
A Backward Glance. New York: Appleton-Century, 1934; New York: Scribner's, 1964.
Eternal Passion in English Poetry. New York: D. Appleton-Century, 1939. With Robert Norton and Gordon Lapsley. Preface by Edith Wharton.

SECONDARY SOURCES

AUCHINCLOSS, LOUIS. *Edith Wharton.* Minneapolis: University of Minnesota Press, 1961. Brief critical account with informed judgments.
———. "Edith Wharton and Her New Yorks," *Partisan Review,* XVIII (1951), 411 - 19. Also in Auchincloss, *Reflections of a Jacobite.* Boston: Houghton Mifflin, 1961, pp. 11 - 28, and Irving Howe, *Edith Wharton,* Englewood Cliffs: Prentice-Hall, 1962. Compares the New Yorks of her three major novels. Sees her succumbing to vulgarity after 1920.
———. *Edith Wharton, A Woman in Her Time.* New York: Viking Press, 1971. Readable biography with excellent pictures.
BEACH, JOSEPH WARREN. *The Twentieth-Century Novel.* New York: Appleton-Century-Crofts, 1932. In "The Well-Made Novel" discusses Edith Wharton's use of point of view in her major novels.

BELL, MILLICENT. *Edith Wharton and Henry James: The Story of Their Friendship.* New York: George Braziller, 1965. Full account of the relationship of Edith Wharton and Henry James. Uses correspondence of both writers.

BERNARD, KENNETH. "Imagery and Symbolism in *Ethan Frome*," *College English*, XXIII (1961), 178 - 84. Excellent article.

BRENNAN, JOSEPH. "Ethan Frome: Structure and Metaphor," *Modern Fiction Studies*, VII (1961), 347 - 56. Excellent article suggesting that narrator and Frome merge into single point-of-view character.

BRENNI, VITO J. *Edith Wharton: A Bibliography*, Morgantown: McClain Printing Co., 1966.

BROWN, E. K. "Edith Wharton," *Etudes Anglaises*, II (1938), 16 - 26. Also in Howe, *Edith Wharton*, pp. 62 - 72. Interesting but judgment that little of her work will endure is dubious.

———. "Edith Wharton: The Art of the Novel," in Pelham Edgar, *The Art of the Novel*. New York: Macmillan, 1933.

———. *Etude Critique*. Lyde-Paris: Librairie E. Droz, 1935. Full-length study (348 pp.). In scope and depth, anticipates the book-length critical studies of Nevius and Walton.

BUCHAN, ALEXANDER. "Edith Wharton and 'The Elusive Bright-Winged Thing,'" *New England Quarterly*, XXXVII (1964), 343-62. Informed article; stresses importance of Weston in *Hudson River Bracketed* for expression of Wharton's views on literature.

CANBY, HENRY SEIDEL. *Definitions*. New York: Harcourt, Brace, 1922. Pp. 212 - 16 on *The Age of Innocence*. Views her dominant concerns as the family and "bourgeois puritanism."

CLOUGH, DAVID. "Edith Wharton's War Novels: A Reappraisal," *Twentieth Century Literature*, XIX (Jan., 1973), 1 - 14. Suggests that her fear of change in French society shocked Edith Wharton more than did her contact with the war. Her desperate stand against change prevented her from achieving accuracy and perspective.

COXE, LOUIS O. "What Edith Wharton Saw in Innocence," *New Republic* (June 27, 1955), pp. 16 - 18. Also Howe, *Edith Wharton*, pp. 155 - 61. Excellent. Stresses the irony involved in the conventional May Welland's being the most heroic character.

EDEL, LEON. *Henry James, the Master: 1901 - 1916.* New York: Lippincott, 1972. Details of friendship with Henry James.

HOPKINS, VIOLA. "The Ordering Style of *The Age of Innocence*," *American Literature*, XXX (1958), 345 - 57. Detailed study of style and its relationship to meaning of the novel.

HOWE, IRVING. ed. *Edith Wharton: A Collection of Critical Essays*. Englewood Cliffs: Prentice-Hall, 1962. Includes next two items below.

———. "Introduction: The Achievement of Edith Wharton," pp. 1 - 18. Also in *Encounter*, XIX (1962), 45 - 52. Emphasizes the range of her achievement and differences between her and James.

————. "A Reading of *The House of Mirth*," pp. 119 - 129. Also appears as introduction to *The House of Mirth.* New York: Holt, Rinehart and Winston, 1962. Excellent commentary.

JAMES, HENRY. *The Art of the Novel.* New York: Scribner's, 1934. Helpful introduction to the prefaces, by R. P. Blackmur.

————. ed. Percy Lubbock, *Letters.* 2 vols. New York: Scribner's, 1920.

————. *Notes on Novelists.* New York: Scribner's, 1914. Contains discussion of *The Custom of the Country.*

KAZIN, ALFRED. "Edith Wharton and Theodore Dreiser," *On Native Grounds.* New York: Reynal and Hitchcock, 1943. Also partly reprinted in Howe, *Edith Wharton*, pp. 89 - 94. Stimulating account; praises Wharton for her tragic sense and for her esthetic force though she remained, in his view, an alien to the American literary scene.

KELLOGG, GRACE. *The Two Lives of Edith Wharton.* New York: Appleton-Century, 1965. Relates Edith Wharton's life as a society matron to her art. Chiefly valuable for letters to Louis Bromfield, 1932 - 36, showing her late views.

LEACH, NANCY R. "Edith Wharton's Unpublished Novel," *American Literature*, XXV (1953), 334 - 53. Describes manuscripts of *Literature: Man of Genius.*

LEAVIS, Q. D. "Henry James' Heiress: The Importance of Edith Wharton," *Scrutiny*, VII (1938), 261 - 76. Also in Howe, *Edith Wharton*, pp. 73 - 88. Sees her as social critic and historian, as well as novelist, who modified James's techniques to reach more readers.

LEWIS, R. W. B. *Edith Wharton.* New York: Harper and Row, 1975, Definitive biography. Uses papers previously unavailable to scholars. Invaluable. Detailed. Objective.

————. "Introduction," *The Collected Short Stories of Edith Wharton.* 2 vols. Boston: Houghton Mifflin, 1971. Incisive account of stories considered in thematic groups. Includes some stories available only in original magazine printing.

LOVETT, ROBERT MORSS. *Edith Wharton.* New York: R. M. McBride, 1925. Early book-length critical study on Wharton.

LUBBOCK, PERCY. "The Novels of Edith Wharton," *Quarterly Review* (London), CCXXIV (Jan., 1915), 182 - 201. Also in Howe, *Edith Wharton*, pp. 43 - 61. Full and appreciative comments on all Wharton works to 1913; stresses Wharton's ironic perspective.

————. *Portrait of Edith Wharton.* New York: Appleton-Century-Crofts, 1947. Informal memoir by a friend.

LYDE, MARILYN. *Edith Wharton: Convention and Morality in the Work of a Novelist.* Norman: Oklahoma University Press, 1959. Thorough account presenting Edith Wharton's views on changing social conventions in light of her persistent moral philosophy.

MAC CALLAN, W. P. "The French Draft of *Ethan Frome*," *Yale Library Gazette*, XXVII (July, 1952), 38 - 47. Full analysis.

MC DOWELL, MARGARET B. "Edith Wharton's 'After Holbein': A Paradigm of the Human Condition," *Journal of Narrative Technique*, I (Spring, 1971), 49 - 58. Detailed analysis.

————. "Edith Wharton's Ghost Tales," *Criticism*, XII (Spring, 1970), 133 - 51. Argues that Edith Wharton in her tales of the supernatural achieved more than her stated aim to send a chill up the spine. Sees profound psychological and moral implications in these stories.

————. "Viewing the Custom of Her Country: Edith Wharton's Feminism," *Contemporary Literature*, XV (Autumn, 1974), 521 - 38.

NEVIUS, BLAKE. *Edith Wharton: A Study of Her Fiction*. Berkeley: University of California Press, 1953, 1961. Excellent critique. Stresses two themes: the sensitive individual is destroyed by lesser people, and he experiences a conflict between his desire for individual freedom and the need to assume social responsibility.

PLANTE, PATRICIA B. "The Critical Reception of Edith Wharton's Fiction in America and England with an Annotated Enumerated Bibliography of Wharton Criticism from 1900 to 1961." Unpublished doctoral dissertation. Boston University, 1962. Discusses reviews and critical articles through 1961.

POIRIER, RICHARD. "Edith Wharton, *The House of Mirth*." Wallace Stegner, ed., *The American Novel from James Fenimore Cooper to William Faulkner*. New York: Basic Books, 1965. Pp. 117 - 132. Excellent critique; relates the novel to the work of Jane Austen and George Eliot.

RANSOM, JOHN CROWE. "Characters and Character," *American Review*, VI (1936), 271 - 88. Critical of Mrs. Wharton's use of narrator in *Ethan Frome*.

RIDEOUT, WALTER B. "Edith Wharton's *The House of Mirth*" in Charles Shapiro, ed. *Twelve Original Essays on Great American Novels*. Detroit: Wayne State University Press, 1958. Pp. 148 - 176. Excellent analysis of structure.

THOMAS, J. D. "Marginalia on *Ethan Frome*," *American Literature*, XXVII (1955), 405 - 09. Notes discrepancies in Mrs. Wharton's use of detail.

TRILLING, DIANA. "*The House of Mirth* Revisited," *Harper's Bazaar*, LXXXI (1947), 126 - 7, 181 - 86. Revised version in Howe, *Edith Wharton*, pp. 108 - 18. Wharton's view of American social history based on the America she knew best informs the novel. Alleges that Selden is modeled on Henry James.

TUTTLETON, JAMES W. "Edith Wharton: An Essay in Bibliography," *Resources for American Literary Study* (Fall, 1973), 163 - 202. Many listings under these headings: Bibliography, Editions, Manuscripts and letters, Biography, and Criticism. Section on criticism (23pp.) briefly annotates essays and reviews, employing first a chronological sampling and later a listing according to topics or individual works.

WALTON, GEOFFREY. *Edith Wharton: A Critical Interpretation*. Teaneck: Fairleigh Dickinson University Press, 1970. Full discussion of works.

Detailed criticism. Indispensable. Avoids adapting his conclusions to assumptions held by previous critics of Edith Wharton. Provides fresh evaluation.

WILSON, EDMUND. "Justice to Edith Wharton," *New Republic*, XCV (1938), 209 - 13. Also in *The Wound and the Bow*, Boston: Houghton Mifflin, 1941, 1947, pp. 195 - 213, and in Howe, *Edith Wharton*, pp. 19 - 31. Important for the revival of critical interest in Edith Wharton, though Wilson thought her career important only between 1905 and 1920.

WOLFF, CYNTHIA. "Lily Bart and the Beautiful Death," *American Literature*, XLVI (March, 1974), 16 - 40. Like the female figures who were idealized in American painting in 1905, Lily Bart faces the impossible demand that women possess asexual and spiritualized beauty in a materialistic society. As a decorative object, Lily is dehumanized by existing only as she is mirrored in the eyes of others.

Index

Renoir, Jean, 39
Repplier, Agnes, 29
Rodin, Auguste, 39
Roosevelt, Theodore, 29, 39

Sand, George, 22
Santayana, George, 39
Scribner's, 33, 43
Sherman, Stuart P., 40, 95
Sinclair, Upton, 53
Stravinsky, Igor, 39
Sturgis, Howard, 31, 32

Tyler, Mrs. Royall, 38

Walton, Geoffrey, 141
Wharton, Edith: burial, 24; Characteristics of work: breadth of work, 40 - 42, 142 - 44; development of the artist, 86, 106, 124f; naturalism, 51, 84, 108, 128 - 29; realism, 103, 107 - 109, 143 - 44; supernatural element in fiction, 86, 87, 91; theory of writing, 84, 85, 108 - 109, 126 - 29; Divorce and expatriation, 26 - 27; marriage, 20; Residences: "Lands End" (Newport), 22; The Mount (Lenox, Mass.), 20, 21, 23, 26, 32, 38, 53, 65; Pavilon Colombe (St. Brin-sons-Foret), 21, 22, 24, 40; Rue de Varenne (Paris apartment), 21, 22, 32, 40, 53; Ste. Claire du Vieux Chateau (Hyeris), 21, 22, 40; Women in society, 25 - 26, 56; War relief: work in Paris, 38 - 40; Accueil Franco-Americain, 38 - 39; Children of Flanders Rescue Committee, 39; Honors: Cross of the Legion of Honor, 39; Gold Medal of Am. Soc. of Arts and Letters, 40; Pulitzer Prize, 41, 95; honorary doctorate from Yale University, 26, 38, 40

WORKS — NON-FICTION:
Backward Glance, A, 19, 23, 27, 34, 47, 53, 64 - 65, 105
Book of the Homeless, The, 39, 110
Decoration of Houses, The, 20, 22, 27
Fighting France, 39, 110
French Ways and Their Meaning, 110
"Great American Novel, The," 109

In Morocco, 38, 39
Italian Backgrounds, 27
Italian Villas and Their Gardens, 27
Motor Flight Through France, A, 32, 38
Writing of Fiction, The, 34, 37, 42, 84, 108

SHORT STORIES:
"After Holbein," 42, 86 - 87, 90 - 91
"All Souls," 42, 86
"Atrophy," 86
"Autres Temps," 87
"Bewitched," 42, 86 - 90
"Bottle of Perrier, The," 42, 86
"Day of the Funeral, The," 42, 86, 87
"Diagnosis," 87
"Eyes, The," 86 - 88
"Fullness of Life," 87
"Her Son," 42
"Journey, A," 85
"Joy in the House," 86, 87
"Lady's Maid's Bell, The," 85
"Lamp of Psyche, The," 87
"Letters, The," 87
"Line of Least Resistance, The," 31
"Miss Mary Pask," 86
"Mission of Jane, The," 85
"Other Two, The," 85
"Pomegranate Seed," 42, 86, 87
"Quicksand, The," 85, 87
"Reckoning, The," 87
"Roman Fever," 42, 86, 87
"Son's Belated," 85, 87
"Triumph of Night, The," 90

NOVELLAS:
Bunner Sisters, 64, 71 - 72
Ethan Frome, 23, 30, 37, 40, 56, 64 - 71, 73, 89, 90, 142
Madame de Treymes, 30, 36, 53, 56 - 57, 140
Marne, The, 39, 110
Old New York, 40, 41, 105
Summer, 40, 64 - 65, 69 - 71, 107, 142

NOVELS:
Age of Innocence, The, 23, 30, 40, 42, 59, 63, 86, 92 - 104, 105, 106, 137, 139, 142

813.52
W 553

99368